I0706958

Guilty

Before Proven Innocent

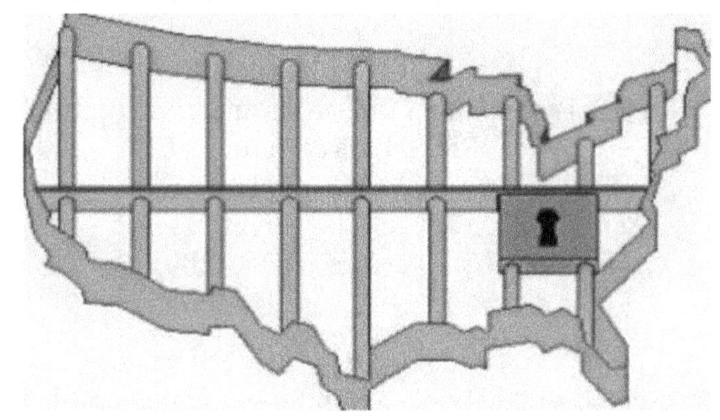

Life Behind America's

Iron Curtain

C.W. Pickett

God Bless America

Where you see wrong or inequality or injustice,
Speak out…
because this is your country.

Make it. Protect it. Pass it on.

United States Supreme Court Justice, Thurgood Marshall

CONTENTS

FORETHOUGHTS

This book is a look into the lives of people living in America in 2019.

Have you ever been convicted of a crime? Then you know about the monkey on your back, the past that haunts your present and your future. You apply for a good-paying job and you do not get it because of your past. You try to rent a nice house, and the landlords refuse to rent to you because of your past.

With 1:38 Americans under control of the U.S. correctional system – more than any other country – too many of us know about that monkey. Sixty-five million need not apply, that is how many qualified workers are lost to the job market because of a tangle with the law.

The burning question that began nearly a year's-worth of research was this: "Is there a connection between poverty, incarceration, and suicide?"

Eleven million Americans experience the "jail churn" yearly. At any given time, there are 2.3 million people behind prison bars, but because of the shorter stays, jails house three to four times as many people as prisons. It is true. "Jail is a hellhole." Dehumanizing. We treat criminals the same way we did 100 years ago. Throw them in a cell and ignore them. Criminals do not have rights, but we fool ourselves into thinking they do because we have not personally experienced America's unjust justice system.

Personal experience with the system has changed my perspective from one of thinking it is fair, to one of knowing for certain it is not fair at all. The intent here is to challenge your perceptions on how you think the U.S. correctional system works. I can say in all certainty, the picture presented here is nothing new for millions of American citizens.

The final section is about innocent people who are convicted and sent to prison. They are there because of misinformation or misidentification. Imagine the impact on the life of someone who is wrongfully accused and in prison for murder, for instance. How do they wake up every morning to a 6 x 8 cell, knowing they are falsely imprisoned, and no one will listen.

Once you hit the legal trail, your life quickly spins downhill, the spiral never stopping. If you had money, a job, and a life before you went in, welcome to the poor house when you get out!

The non-convicted awaiting trial cannot afford their bond or bail and so they sit. A speedy trial happens within six-months' time. When the court dockets are overloaded, the wait can be longer than the sentence. After a while, the accused will give up and take a plea agreement and a lesser sentence, just to get it over with.

Punishment is for serious crimes; murder, rape, drug trafficking, and the like; but women are incarcerated at an amazing rate for low misdemeanors! They break a minor law, get arrested, fail their probation, and end up in jail. Their children suffer. The cycle begins.

Society keeps people in their roles of poverty through income inequality, scarcity of services, and incarceration. There are better ways to deal with America's wayward citizens. Most of them are on a rough stretch, doing what they can to survive. Homeless people go to jail for panhandling or sleeping in their cars. Why is that necessary? Is it illegal to be homeless?

Just as the question arises, is it illegal to have a mental illness? Our jails are a holding cell for the mentally ill. "Mentally ill" has a stigma that carries the same implications as "formerly incarcerated." Just as we categorize what an ex-con is like, we carry an image of jails full of ravaged, wild-eyed waifs who yell crazy insanities. Most behavior and emotional difficulties (i.e., mental illnesses) are related to maltreatment as a child. The jails are full of women who have been sexually molested as children, but rather than treatment, we offer incarceration.

Keep in mind that the states that spend the least on mental health services spend the most on corrections. As a case in point, Wyoming, which ranks #13 in the <u>world</u> for incarceration, spends $300 million a year on corrections. A one-time $10 million is allocated for suicide prevention.

Jails hold more people with mental health illnesses than any psychiatric hospital in the country. Does sitting in jail make you crazy? If you have post-traumatic stress or schizophrenia, anxiety, or panic attacks, a jail is not the best place to be relaxing and having a good time!

WHY JAIL IS BAD FOR YOUR HEALTH

1. The lights are on 24/7. Day in, day out, there is halogen and/or fluorescent lighting in the day room, the sleeping rooms, and the exercise yard. This is light torture. The body needs dark to process melatonin for sleep. The mind and body need a restful nights' sleep to function properly.

2. The food is meant to tempt empty bellies, and not intended to be wildly nutritious or balanced. A poor diet contributes to mental-health problems as much as lack of sleep.

3. Hygiene. Shared toilet facilities, improper sanitation, less-than-clean conditions, all of these contribute to the rampant spread of disease.

4. Lack of sunshine or exercise. You can be sure the jailers do not pass out vitamin D pills! Without sunshine, depression sets in. Jails do not promote much activity, and we know what lack of activity does to our bodies.

It is true, people are in jail to be punished, but why does punishment take away basic human needs? If proper food, exercise, sunshine, and adequate hygiene were provided, jail would not be such a hellhole.

SPEAKING OF LIVING IN HELL…

Statistics show you will die by your own hand before you will die by someone else's!

Suicide is more prevalent in America than murder. Second to accidental deaths, suicide is the second cause of death for people aged 15 to 24. Pre-teens and teenagers are the highest group at risk for suicidal thoughts and intentions.

***The rates of suicide and incarceration have steadily risen, side-by-side,
for the last thirty years.***

How does a person get to the bottom of the barrel, to be in such despair that they choose to take their life? How does a person get to the bottom of the barrel to begin with?

Incarceration and suicide are inversely related to poverty, but poverty is not necessarily an indicator of suicide. Victims have both the lowest incomes and the highest incomes.

We consider a person who commits suicide to be mentally ill. We assume a person in jail is a bad person and deserves to be punished.

If this is what you believe, be prepared for a shock! Perhaps even raise your blood pressure a notch or two!   People should not be treated in such a manner, especially in a county that claims "freedom" as their password.

RESOURCES

There are bits and pieces of the puzzle, but no single source addresses the complete picture of suicide, incarceration, and poverty. The causal relationships between the three are hinted at in various reports, and it is in this book where we combine the facts of these issues. What transpires is a troubling picture of the American family.

Most of the data on the states came from the Annie E. Casey Foundation Kids Count Databook 2019 and the Robert Wood Johnson Foundation County Health Rankings 2018. The Department of Justice supplied the prison rates, and the Center for Disease Control and Prevention provided the information on suicide.

The statistical information is provided to give you a clear picture of the situation. Data on the states varies slightly from year to year. Rather than haggle over slight discrepancies in numbers, the idea here is to present an overview of the total picture.

Six of the ten states within the Suicide Belt rank in the top twenty for both the highest incarceration _and_ suicide rates. Does the rural nature of these states and the lack of healthcare have anything to do with it? Or is there more to this picture?

Here is where we attempt to answer these questions and spread some light on the plight of one-third of American citizens locked behind this Iron Curtain called incarceration.

If what you read makes you uncomfortable, or you hear yourself saying "No, way can that be!" please take a moment and consider that "Yes, it is possible 'that can be!'"

I use the quotes of Malcom X, a leader of the social revolution in the 1960's, because what he says is as true today as they were then. He advocated for liberating the Black people, but it is fair to say discrimination knows no color in today's world. People should have listened to the flower children, the tree huggers, the Malcolms of the world, who told us to straighten up and fly right. They saw the destructive path this world was headed and look at us now.

Americans take our freedom seriously and come through a crisis a bit dusty and shaken, but always victorious. No other country has enjoyed the amenities of freedom like we have, but you cannot miss the irony that more Americans are behind bars than the Communist countries!

After we lay the groundwork and get the details out of the way, the story becomes more interesting. To begin with, we visit the topics of suicide and incarceration. We then address the impact on ethnic groups, families, and women and children; and how certain states report on these measures. Lastly, we take a close look at one state, Wyoming, the Equality State. This motto is rather tongue in cheek, considering the state was the first political entity in the <u>world</u> to give women the right to vote in 1869, and in 2019 ranks second in the <u>world</u> for incarcerating women.

We end the book with a famous and highly controversial case of a man who was hung for murder but did not commit the crime. Land, cattle, and water – a perfect combination to foster hate and wars that led to lynchings and murders. Tom Horn is a controversial figure because of his guilty conviction. Historians have parsed his life to no end, making him a man that killed seventeen times. This is not the man portrayed here, the man I saw while reading of his predicament. The experts will probably criticize my interpretation of the case of Tom Horn, but there are no excuses for the deputy that wrongly arrested him, the prosecutor that wrongly convicted him, or the governor that condemned an innocent man to death.

PART I

A NATION IN TROUBLE

I believe that it is possible for Brotherhood to be brought about among all people, but I do not delude myself into dreaming or falling for a dream that this exists before it exists...Some of the leaders of our people in this country...say...they believe in a dream. But while they are dreaming, our people are having a nightmare.

Malcolm X
Interview with Les Crane, December 27, 1964

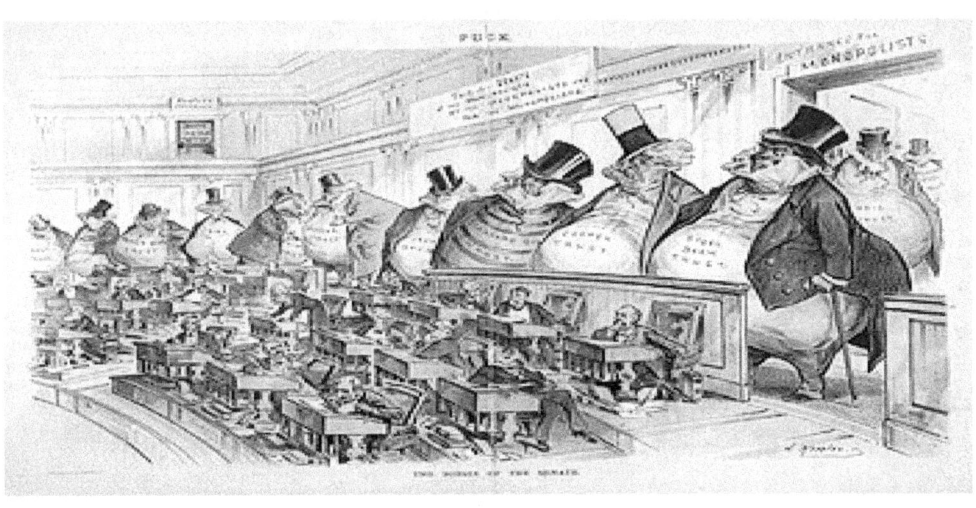

Chapter 1

GOOD-BYE, CRUEL WORLD

Suicide has always been with us, and always will be. In some cultures, it is an honorable thing to take your life. The Japanese kamikaze pilots in World War II knew exactly what they were doing and flew to their deaths willingly. Several cultures have the equivalent of "losing face," a deep embarrassment or shame, and remedy this by "falling on their sword."

Our American culture does not view suicide in the same way, however. For many years, the act of suicide was illegal, but the only people that paid for the crime were the ones who failed their attempt! We pity the family because one of their members could not hold it together. "There must be something seriously wrong with them," we whisper.

Once we look at the facts behind suicide, though, perhaps you will realize the trouble is not with the family itself, but the way our society treats those who are in need. We ostracize and condemn people who are not "like" us. Discrimination is inbred into our culture. It is natural for us to hate, to be angry, to show violence.

Industrial countries have higher rates of suicides than non-industrialized countries, and the United States is somewhere in the middle. The official final data on suicidology shows 47,173 people died in 2017 - meaning one person dies every 11.1 minutes (Drapeau & McIntosh, 2018).

Suicide is a horrible shock to those left behind. Most people do not see it coming. We tend to not address someone's distress unless they approach us. When someone we know is a tattered mess, we turn away and pretend to ignore them. And then, the next day, "I just saw them yesterday!"

There is usually not a clue the person was ready to take his life. At least clues we do not see, until hindsight sets in. One suicide has far-reaching repercussions. Six people are directly affected by one death, and 147 people are indirectly affected, or 6.9 million people each year. Half of the population knows of someone who committed suicide during their lifetime (Drapeau & McIntosh, 2018).

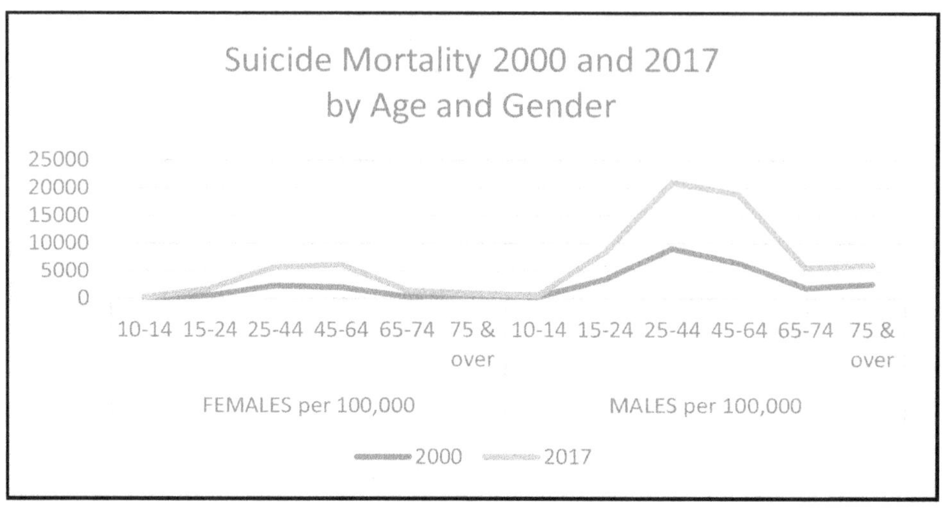

Sources: *Data Brief. 330. Suicide Mortality in the U.S. 1999-2017.* NCHS.
Data Brief 309. *Suicide rates in the U.S. continue to increase. 2000-2016.* NCHS.

WHO COMMITS SUICIDE?

This is the formula used for statistical data on suicide, incarceration, and poverty:

***The number of suicides in a group, divided by the number of people in a group,
multiplied by 100,000, equals Rate of Suicide***
(Number of suicides/number of people x 100,000 = Rate)
Drapeau & McIntosh

Rate is the gauge used for comparison of statistical data when measuring groups of people.   The larger the group, the lower the rate.   Young adult males have the highest <u>number</u> of suicides yet rank lower than white males 75 years old and older. Older males have the highest suicide <u>rate</u> of any age group because the group of older men is smaller, and they commit suicide more often.

Here are the facts on who commits suicide:

- Men commonly have co-occurring alcohol and substance use disorders – men frequently are not recognized as having problems and do not seek treatment.

- Men use lethal methods such as firearms, carbon monoxide poisoning, hanging, or jumping from a height.

- Women attempt suicide more often than men, but are less likely to carry it out.

- Women ages 44 to 64 have the highest rates for their gender.

20

- Suicide ranks second highest for adolescents and young adults between the ages of 15 and 24, with homicide as the third leading cause.

- People in rural areas generally use a firearm. The distance to travel for emergency care and the inability to get immediate help makes firearms the most lethal means of suicide.

- Economic status is not a predictor; both the lowest-low and the highest-high incomes are associated with suicide.

- Some occupations may carry a higher risk for suicide, but there is not enough evidence to prove whether police officers, dentists, or psychiatrists commit suicide more frequently than people in other occupations

- The weapon of choice for Caucasian males, ages 75 and up, is a firearm (Suicide Stats, 2019).

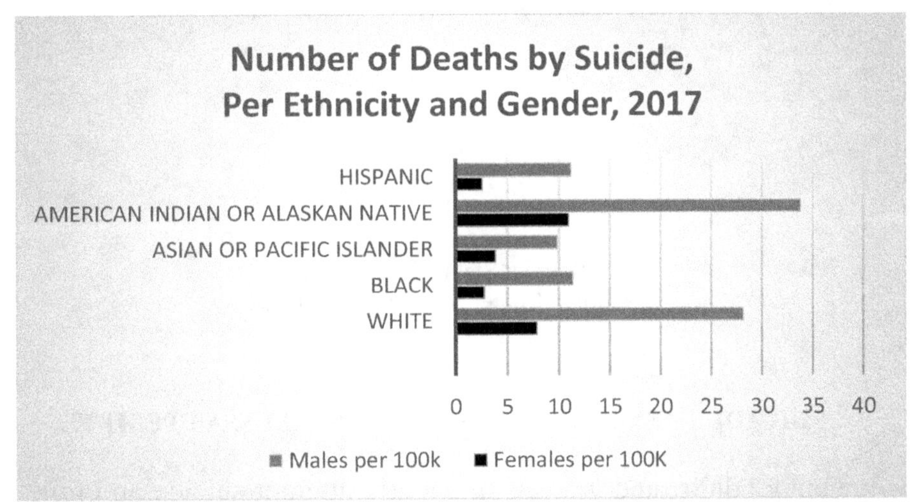

Curtain & Hedegaard. *Suicide Rates for females and males by race and ethnicity.*
National Center for Health Statistics.

As we look for patterns as to why people commit suicide, the first question is why are the states with the highest suicide rates clustered within the Mountain States? Except for Alaska, the states that fit this pattern are referred to as the Suicide Belt, represented by the states in the figure "The Suicide Belt" in dark grey. These states are within the top twenty for suicides, and the bottom ten for health well-being. Some states do better with child well-being than others.

Apart from Oklahoma and Alaska, all the high-ranking suicide states are in the Mountain region. What do these states have in common? They are all rural. They are the largest states per square mile in the country, they have the lowest population per square mile, except

Colorado, and have the largest concentration of population in the larger cities. The states with the highest suicide rates rank the lowest in health well-being. As we will see, there are several reasons why these states rank as they do. The answer is complex. Inadequate healthcare is only one of the contributions to suicide.

THE SUICIDE BELT

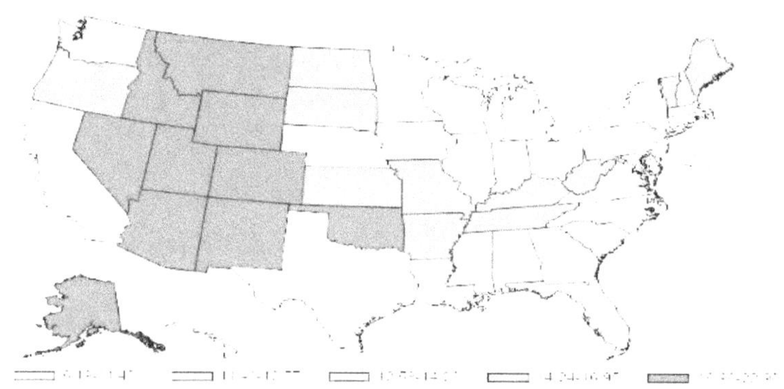

Source: Stats of the States
National Center for Health Statistics

SUICIDE IDEATION AND UNSUCCESSFUL ATTEMPTS

Teenagers, young adults, and women frequently attempt suicide and fail. Attempts are regarded as a cry for help, and our youth are crying out. Do we hear them? In a report by the CDC, *Stats of the States,* a survey of high school students revealed:

- seriously considered suicide in the last year – 16%
- created a plan – 13%
- attempted suicide – 8%
- 157,000 youth ages 10-25 are seen in the emergency room every year for self-inflicted injuries

Youth violence is running rampant in our country today; one out of five students are bullied on any given day; 160,000 children stay home from school each day to avoid their bully (Pickett, 2019). Is daily exposure to violence the cause of youth suicides?

Table 1. Rankings for suicide, health, and overall child well-being in the Suicide Belt.

2019 RANKINGS FOR STATES IN THE SUICIDE BELT, INCLUDING ALASKA[1]									
SUICIDE[1]									
MT	AK	WY	NM	ID	UT	CO	NV	OK	AZ
1	2	3	4	5	6	10	11	14	20
HEALTH WELL-BEING[2]									
44	50	49	48	23	21	41	46	43	35
OVERALL CHILD WELL-BEING[2]									
22	45	21	50	18	7	20	47	42	47
Source: [1]Sawyer. (2019). *U.S. States with the highest suicide rates.* [2]Kids Count Data Center, 2019									
KEY FOR ABBREVIATION OF STATES **MT**- Montana; **AK**- Alaska; **WY**-Wyoming; NM-New Mexico; **ID**-Idaho; **UT**-Utah; **CO**-Colorado; **NV**-Nevada; **OK**-Oklahoma; **AZ**-Arizona									

+

REASONS FOR SUICIDE

A major life crisis can ruin a person's chances to form healthy social connections and support. If someone in crisis has established resilient characteristics, such as a supportive family, religiosity, and a sound community network, they will come through their crisis better than before. But for someone in a crisis who does not have the support they need, their life spirals downhill, sometimes to the point where they cannot cope any longer.

One event does not trigger suicide. The risk of suicide compounds with too many of these "reasons" happening at once.

The CDC lists these as the common reasons for suicide (Vital):

- Relationship difficulties (42%)
- A major crisis (29%)
- Alcohol and drug use (28%)

- Issues with physical health (22%)
- Job/financial setbacks (16%)
- Incarceration/legal issues (9%)
- Housing instability (loss of housing, homelessness) (4%).

People have more than one thing going on in their life if they are to the point of giving up. As we will see in the next chapter, incarceration can cause serious life problems, resulting in multiple reasons to want to die.

It is easy to see how someone in incredible pain gives up. Thousands of Americans give testament to how uncontrollable pain has taken over their lives. Sleep deprivation is a great stumbling block for psychological and physical health – one with depression cannot sleep; lack of sleep keeps you tired all day; depression comes from being tired; and the cycle goes 'round and 'round.

> We claim that someone who commits suicide must be "crazy," depressed and suicidal, but interestingly, only half of the victims see a mental health counselor and carry a mental health diagnosis – and half of those commit suicide while they are in counselling! The other half of the victims show no outward signs, or at least do not have a mental health diagnosis. But this group also does not seek counseling, which makes it impossible to guess if there was a mental disorder before the suicide.
> (Kovner & Knickman, 2008)

How does it work? Does someone one day just give up, pull out a gun on a whim, and shoot himself? Victims of suicide struggle for years, fighting with their pain and depression – and their post-traumatic-stress.

PERCEIVED BURDENSOMENESS AND THWARTED BELONGINGNESS

Along the line of thinking that it takes years to get to the point of suicide, Dr. Thomas Joiner, author of *Why People Die by Suicide,* posits an interesting theory. He believes there are only three motives for suicide.

1. A sense of burden to others
2. A profound sense of loneliness
3. A sense of fearlessness

All three of these preconditions must be in place before the person is ready to commit suicide. So long as a person remains fearful of death and the consequences of the actions that lead to death, they will not take their life.

Over time, people who ruminate on dying become habituated to having no fear of death, making them immune to the horrors of taking their life (Van Nuys).

A feeling of belongingness to a group is essential for human survival. Joiner's first two preconditional signs have a direct connection to belonging. When someone forms the opinion that he is a burden on his loved ones, he withdraws from them, and becomes isolated and lonely. Social isolation, an effect of bullying and other forms of violence, create a disconnect with others and an inability to maintain long-term relationships (Joiner).

Co-occurring depression and PTSD are the most significant correlations for risk of suicide. Exposure to a traumatic event such as childhood maltreatment raises the risk of suicide. Does this exposure eventually erode one is thinking to where they want to die? In some cases, you can see it, such as the child who is bullied.

> *Prevention efforts should not be aimed toward the final hours of despair, but rather helping people resolve their issues before they reach the point of no- return.*

Thinking about dying follows the concept of "your thoughts make you." You are what you think. When in a funk deep enough to want to take your life, you have been on this downhill trend for some time.

AUTOBIOGRAPHICAL MEMORY

Suicide rates rise with age for both men and women, as they become older and feel they are a trouble to their family. Older adults give vague warnings which can be confused with the normal end-of-life planning, such as drawing up wills and giving away personal possessions. They ordinarily do not communicate their intent to die, but instead say things like, "There is nothing left for me anymore." Contributing circumstances are widowhood, serious medical illnesses, and social isolation.

The "remembered self" is a representation of who we have been at various points in our life. We tell stories of our history to gain a sense of identity. As we grow older, we tend to remember our young independent years the most, those ages between 18 and 22 (Broderick & Blewitt, 2010).

We were young, fearless, and the had the world by the tail. This time period is called "the bump" – and our flashbulb memories are especially vivid and personally relevant from this time in our lives.

This is why the elderly reminisce about their favorite books they read, the movies they watched, and the songs they listened to. They refer to the years of their young adulthood more frequently than other times in their lives.

Later on, we talk about childhood trauma and its far-reaching effects. As adults age, a traumatic past becomes more troublesome and harder to process. If the experience occurs during "the bump" years, such as going off to war or being raped in college, then according to the autobiographical memory theory, the memories are more pressing and painful as we get older.   Unresolved trauma causes loneliness and a sense of not belonging. Relationships fail, children leave home never to return, disappointment ensues, and the memories will not abate.

What better recipe for a self-inflicted fatal wound than a life of pain and suffering?

THE TEN LEADING CAUSES OF DEATH ARE PREVENTABLE

If Americans were to live a life of prevention and slow the fast track we are on, we could all live to a ripe old age. Since we do not have healthy lifestyles, here is how we die in the order in which we die:

1. Heart disease
2. Cancer
3. Accidents
4. Chronic respiratory disease
5. Stroke
6. Alzheimer's
7. Diabetes mellitus
8. Influenza and Pneumonia
9. Kidney disease
10. Suicide (Drapeau & McIntosh, 2018)

Humans have an amazing capacity for survival. The clock just does not stop ticking, you cannot flip a switch and turn off your life. We have deep resources of resilience and can withstand the most horrendous experiences.

We will not come out of those experiences the same person we were when we went in, but there is little that can permanently daunt the human spirit. Look back on history and visit the stories of people like Viktor Frankl who withstood the Nazi concentration camps, one of the most inhumane tortures in the history of our world. How do people survive these things – not only survive, but use their experiences as an impetus for changing the world?

Even the most resilient can eventually give out in circumstances that are too stressful to bear. Violence is the destroyer of minds and men. Violence of wars, of families, of society; we are slowly destroying our nation, our families, and communities, because we cannot control the violence.

People are affected by violence in two ways – 1) they turn the anger inside themselves, or 2) they take it out on others. There is one similarity in the psychology behind a mass murderer and a person who commits suicide. Both have reached the end of their rope and they cannot cope with their anger at society and the people who wronged them.

Why do people reach a point in their lives where they feel they cannot take another step forward? Why do people want to give up? Only half the victims of suicide have a diagnosed mental disorder. Is there more contributing to their distress than marital strain or loneliness? I am certainly not debunking these two. But a marriage can be saved, and loneliness can be remedied. There must be more than just an outlook on life, or state of depression, that causes someone to take their life.

Was there ever a time in America when most of the people were happy and were not fraught with such immense challenges at every turn? It is true this is a complicated world. People are having difficulty coping. If we could eliminate just a few of the stressors, our world would be a happier place.

Prejudice and oppression are a part of our culture whether we want to admit it or not. Drugs and crime are also a major part of our culture. Poverty, violence, and injustice will always be among us.

Veterans of Foreign Wars comprise about ten percent of the total U.S. population. We may disagree with the reasons for the war, but everyday men and women put down their lives so we can live in freedom.

Wars have never been pretty, but with modern technology comes deadlier weapons, and deadlier injuries. Standing within percussive range of an IED (improvised explosive device) will, at the least, cause a head injury.

According to Dr. Joiner, exposure to violence inhibits the of fear of dying, which can lead to suicidal tendencies. Do the American veterans who takes their lives at a rate of twenty-two a day support his theory? Exposure to violence in the late teens and early twenties, the age of most soldiers, rewires a brain that is not fully developed. Because of how war affects the mind, it is hard to say what this rewiring does at the time.

Patients who commit suicide in the Veterans Administration system are elderly males with little social support. They have medical and mental conditions consistent with suicide. Their choice of weapon is a firearm (Kaplan et al, 2007). In 2016, veterans over 55 comprised fifty-eight percent of veteran suicides (Facts, 2017).

Suicide of women who have served our country is on the rise. Between 2000 and 2014, the rates of suicides for women in the military increased by two-thirds! Much of this is attributed to military sexual harassment - sexual assault and harassment from coworkers and superiors.

The risk of suicide is two-and-a-half times more for military women than civilian women. Those under age 40 experience a higher suicide rate and use firearms three times more than women in the general population (Facts, 2017).

Generally, veterans take better care of themselves than civilians. They are more physically active, most have health insurance, and most veterans are employed.

Most report insufficient sleep, and consumption of alcohol and tobacco use is about the same as a civilian. Women veterans experience more anxiety, depression, and frequent mental distress than male veterans (Health, 2018).

Veterans experience functional impairment and pain more frequently that their civilian cohorts. Not surprisingly, veterans' attempts at suicide are usually successful, possibly because their knowledge and experience with firearms makes them able to carry out their intent (Health, 2018),

SUICIDE AMONG THE AMERICAN INDIANS AND ALASKAN NATIVES

The Wyoming county that ranks the highest in suicides also has a population that is twenty-two percent American Indian. A quick check into the ethnic groups of the other two top suicidal states revealed that the highest rates were among American Indians/Alaskan Native (AI/AN). The various tribes live mainly in Alaska, Montana, Wyoming, New Mexico, and Arizona, and were 1.5 percent, or 4.5 million, of the U.S. Census in 2018. Table 2 shows the two top counties in Montana, Alaska, and Wyoming for comparison of their minority population and suicides.

The information for suicides is taken from state death certificates, and even though each reservation is a separate country within the U.S., deaths are registered with the state. In 2010, the CDC reported suicide in American Indian and Alaskan Native communities as the eighth leading cause of death, at a rate of 16.92 per 100,000 residents, with the overall national suicide death rate at 12.08.

In the U.S. population, suicide rates increase with age. In the AI/AN population, suicide rates decrease with age, and is the second leading cause of death for ages 5 to 24. The adjusted suicide rate for this age group was 39.7 per 100,000. For the same age group in the overall United States population, the rate was 9.9 per 100,000. Suicide rates for AI/AN males between the ages of 15-24 was 58.7 per 100,000, three-and-one-half times more than the same group in the general population, with a rate of 16.0 per 100,000 people (Suicide).

Poverty Rate among AI/AN: 25.4%
Total Population of AI/AN in poverty: 670,570

Sauter (2018). *Faces of Poverty*

Table 2. Suicide rank and ethnic groups in the three states highest for suicide, by county.

2019 TOP RANKING COUNTIES OF THE SUICIDE STATES						
	Montana		Alaska		Wyoming	
Suicide Rank/Rate per 100K[1]	1 28.94		2 27.01		3 26.94	
Top 2 counties for suicide[2]	Deer Lodge	Rooseve lt	Nome Census Area	Northwes t Arctic Census Area	Fremon t	Hot Spring s
Suicide rank/rate per 100K[2]	1 35.67	2 30.76	1 70.19	2 61.03	1 30.4	2 27.5
% White[3]	92.4	34.7	15.7	12.0	73.8	95.4
% Black[2]	0.4	0.4	0.8	1.6	0.6	0.7
% AI/AN[2]	3.9	60.6	75.5	79.3	22.1	1.6
% Hispanic[2]	3.7	4.2	2.5	3.8	7.0	4.0
Source: [1]Sawyer. (2019). *U.S. States with the highest suicide rates.* [2]Worldlifeexpectancy.com [3]United States Census Bureau. QuickFacts (2019)						

RISK FACTORS AND PROTECTIVE FACTORS FOR THE AI/AN COMMUNITY

Risk and protective factors are individual, community, and environmental circumstances that increase or decrease the likelihood of committing suicide. These can be fixed, such as family history or trauma, or can be changeable, such as drug addiction, alcoholism, and depression (Suicide).

Forced relocation and separation of children from their families to attend school, plus the loss of cultural traditions fosters a sense of not belonging. Hopelessness leads to a disconnection with self and others, and depression invariably follows, and there is no one to talk to who can help sort out troubling relationships and family troubles (Suicide).

The studies conducted of high-risk AI/AN communities found they were rural, with high unemployment and poverty. Clusters of suicide occur around adolescent- or young-adult males with a history of chronic alcohol use, suicide of a family member, unstable family relationships and home life, individual or parental unemployment, and loss of traditional AI/AN language and culture within the community (Curtain & Hedegaard, 2019).

ISOLATED FROM THE WORLD

Isolation is a factor. The town of Nome, Alaska, has a population of 4,000 people, and sits on the coast of the Bearing Strait. There are no roads leading to Nome; the only way to get in or out is by dogsled or airplane (Nome). The Nome Census Area is home to the Inupiat where 9,878 people reside. The poverty rate is 24.9 percent (USA).

Northwest Arctic Borough is the second-largest borough in Alaska, and covers over 36,000 miles of land and water. It is located above the Arctic Circle, and temperatures range from minus 50 in the winter to 85 degrees in the summer (Northwest). The largest town is Katzebu, (population 3,121). Minerals mined in the interior are shipped out from the port of Katzebu (USA). Even with active mineral extraction in the area, the poverty rate is 18.8 percent. The Burrough is also home to the Inupiat tribe. They have been in Alaska since crossing over from the Bearing Strait.

The website for Roosevelt County, Montana says this:

Not far from the Canadian border, Fort Peck Indian Reservation encompasses most of Roosevelt County. There are 7,000 residents of Assiniboine and Sioux descent, with a total population of 10,262 and land area of 2.1 million acres. Thirteen percent of the AI/AN adolescents in Roosevelt County attempted suicide in 2017.

The reservation is rife with alcoholism and drug use. Isolation is prevalent in that one in seven residents have no vehicle, and one in six have no phone. The poverty rate is 29.1 percent (Fort).

Fremont County, Wyoming is the largest of the six counties, with a population of 40,354, and a poverty rate of 13.7 percent. The Wind River Indian Reservation covers 2.2 million acres within Fremont and Hot Springs Counties. The Reservation is home to 9,000 Northern Arapahoe and 4,000 Eastern Shoshoni. As with Fort Peck, drugs and alcohol are a serious problem for the tribes.

TWO COUNTIES THAT DO NOT FIT THE PROFILE OF HIGH AI/AN SUICIDE RATES

	Deer Lodge County, Montana	Hot Springs County, Wyoming
White Population[1]	95.4%	92.4%
Suicide Rates/100,000[2]	36.55	27.54
Total Square Miles[1]	11,218	4,741
Total Population[1]	9,131	4,555
Veterans[1]	10%	13%
Median Age[2]	47	49

Source: [1]*Quickfacts: Wyoming.* Center for Disease Control
[2]*USA causes of death by age and gender (2018).* USA LifeExpectancy

The city of Anaconda is an incorporated city/county government that encompasses the total population of Deer Lodge County. Nestled in the Anaconda Mountains in southwestern Montana close to Yellowstone Park, the closest town is thirty miles away. The long Montana winters and snow-packed roads hinder travel that time of year.

Hot Springs County is home to hot mineral water that attracts visitors from all over the world. It neighbors the ecosystem of Yellowstone Park and contains part of the Wind River Indian Reservation. The closest town is thirty miles away to the north, and winter travel is hazardous through the mountain canyon to the south.

We can pinpoint causes of suicide for the AI/AN communities, but what happens in a small town that feels like Mayberry, USA, on first glance?

Isolation plays a role in suicide in these rural communities, but so does the lack of belongingness. It is easy to lose oneself in the city, but in a small town where everyone knows everyone else's business, some people are ostracized because they do not fit in.

The further from emergency care, the less the chance of surviving an attempt on one's life. Finding professionals in healthcare and mental health who are willing to live in places that are very rural with small populations, wide-open spaces, and far from culture and civilization, is also problematic for these small communities.

Unemployment, poverty, isolation, incarceration, trauma, and homelessness seem to be the cocktail mix for suicide. Not all circumstances need be present. For some people, losing a job is enough to send them over the edge.

GUN CONTROL LAWS

The evidence speaks for individuals at risk of suicide: If there is a gun in the house, they will use it. Case-controlled studies show that there was an increase of suicide in homes where there were guns and risk of suicide, even when adjusted for circumstances such as drug use, education, and criminal history (Kaplan et al, 2008).

Comparison of the states with the highest suicide rates to the states with the lowest rates presents a strong argument for gun control laws. The states with the lowest suicide rates are all populated eastern states. Gun control laws in the Western states are practically nonexistent, because, well, these are western states. Guns are historically a part of the culture, and in some states, there are more guns than people. Interestingly, the suicide states have some of the lowest violent crime rates, despite all the guns.

Barriers prevent people from dying (Joiner). If there are barriers on bridges, people will not jump. A gun lock is a barrier. To use the weapon, you must go through a series of steps – taking the impulse of the moment away – which may be the time needed to reconsider your actions.

Table 3. Comparison of gun control laws between the highest ranking and lowest ranking states.

<table>
<tr><td colspan="10">2019 RANKINGS FOR STATES IN THE SUICIDE BELT, INCLUDING ALASKA</td></tr>
<tr><td colspan="10">SUICIDE[1]</td></tr>
<tr><td>MT</td><td>AK</td><td>WY</td><td>NM</td><td>ID</td><td>UT</td><td>CO</td><td>NV</td><td>OK</td><td>AZ</td></tr>
<tr><td>1</td><td>2</td><td>3</td><td>4</td><td>5</td><td>6</td><td>10</td><td>11</td><td>14</td><td>20</td></tr>
<tr><td colspan="10">GUN CONTROL LAWS IN 2013[2]</td></tr>
<tr><td>N</td><td>N</td><td>N</td><td>N</td><td>N</td><td>OC</td><td>BGC</td><td>N</td><td>OC</td><td>N</td></tr>
<tr><td colspan="10">PERCENT OF SUICIDES BY FIREARM IN 2013[2]</td></tr>
<tr><td>60</td><td>70</td><td>69</td><td>52</td><td>65</td><td>51</td><td>49</td><td>54</td><td>65</td><td>56</td></tr>
<tr><td colspan="10"></td></tr>
<tr><td colspan="10">2019 RANKINGS FOR STATES LOWEST IN SUICIDES</td></tr>
<tr><td colspan="10">SUICIDE[1]</td></tr>
<tr><td>VA</td><td>RI</td><td>DE</td><td>IL</td><td>CA</td><td>CT</td><td>MD</td><td>MA</td><td>NJ</td><td>NY</td></tr>
<tr><td>41</td><td>42</td><td>43</td><td>44</td><td>45</td><td>46</td><td>47</td><td>48</td><td>49</td><td>50</td></tr>
<tr><td colspan="10">GUN CONTROL LAWS IN 2013[2]</td></tr>
<tr><td>N</td><td>WP, BGC, OC</td><td>BGC</td><td>BCG, OC</td><td>WP, BGC, GL, OC</td><td>BGC, GL, OC</td><td>WP, BGC, OC</td><td>WP, BGC, OC</td><td>WP, BGC OC</td><td>BGC, GL, OC</td></tr>
<tr><td colspan="10">PERCENT OF SUICIDES BY FIREARMS IN 2013[2]</td></tr>
<tr><td>56</td><td>26</td><td>49</td><td>38</td><td>39</td><td>28</td><td>45</td><td>20</td><td>26</td><td>28</td></tr>
<tr><td colspan="10"></td></tr>
</table>

KEY FOR GUN LAWS

N – no gun laws, **WP** – Waiting Period, **BGC** – Background Check, **GL** – Gun Locks, **OC** -Open Carry

KEY FOR ABBREVIATION OF STATES

MT- MONTANA; **AK**- ALASKA; **WY**-WYOMING; **NM**-NEW MEXICO; **ID**-IDAHO; **UT**-UTAH; **CO**-COLORADO; **NV**-NEVADA; **OK**-OKLAHOMA; **AZ**-ARIZONA

VA – VIRGINIA; **RI** – RHODE ISLAND; **DE** – DELAWARE; **IL** – ILLINOIS; **CA** – CALIFORNIA; **CT** – CONNECTICUT; **MD** – MARYLAND; **MA** – MASSACHUSETTS; **NJ** – NEW JERSEY; **NY** – NEW YORK

Source: [1]Sawyer. (2019). *U.S. States with the highest suicide rates.*
[2]Anestis & Anestis. *Suicide rates and state laws regulating access and exposure to handguns.*

Chapter 2

AMERICA – THE WORLD-LEADER FOR INCARCERATION

The subtitle for my book, *Life behind America's Iron Curtain*, is intentionally aimed at the *justice* system that rules over countless Americans in the form of iron bars that enclose jail and prison cells. The annual number of Americans in prison is 2.3 million. This does not count the 10 or 11 million people caught up in the "jail churn."   It is called the "churn" because stays are shorter, and more people pass through jails than federal or state prisons.

We throw people in jail for everything – and for nothing. Someone has a mental health melt down, we do not know what else to do with them, so we throw them in jail. A mother is arrested for possession of a small amount of marijuana and finds herself sentenced to six months' jail time. A boy graduates from high school with a new life ahead of him and is convicted for fighting with his buddy. His plans for his future are dashed. Is it necessary to jail people for minor offenses?

An encounter with the law can follow a person around for the rest of their life. A criminal sentence will keep them from renting a house, finding a good-paying job, or getting a loan at the bank. Once caught in the churn it is difficult to get out. The cycle of poverty and incarceration spins like a lost wheel rolling down the road.

What lies behind this iron curtain called incarceration? Americans not involved within the judicial system think everything works as it should. We are naïve until it happens to us. In an attempt to purge some of that naivety, here is a look into the lives of people who live behind those bars.

AMERICA, THE FREE, OR NOT SO FREE FOR MANY

First of all, let us get the mundane facts out of the way. In the United States, 1:37 adults are under correctional control; people in jails and prisons, and community supervision (probation and parole} (Jones, 2018).

***The United States of America has five percent of the
world's total population***

*ved***AND is the world leader in incarcerating it citizens.***

2.3 million Americans are in prison

11 million Americans are in jail

4.5 million Americans are on probation/parole

Each Year...

The U.S. has had the highest incarceration rate in the world since 2002. If all the people on probation and parole were grouped into one state, there would be enough people for the sixteenth largest state in the nation! (Jones, 2018). The size of South Dakota.

America ranks #1 in the world for incarceration, but places #24 when compared to the states, if every state was considered a country. These states are incarcerating their citizens at a faster rate than the U.S.

You would think those states with high incarceration rates would have the highest violent crime, but except for Alaska, New Mexico, and Nevada, this is not the case. Oklahoma ranks #14 in both incarceration and violent crime, and #1 in the world for incarceration. As you read along, keep your eye on Oklahoma.

Before the War on Drugs, if you murdered someone, you went to prison for life, or met the death penalty. There have always been illegal drugs, but the dealers went to jail, not their victims.   Those where the days when a person could roam free and not have to worry which crime he might be committing. All you had to do was obey the law, and you knew what the laws were. You rarely knew an "ex-con," and if you did, you did not associate with them. Today, it seems everyone you meet has a criminal record of some sort – at least that is the way it is in my state.

There are more laws on the books today than ever before in our history. Lawmakers take their job title too seriously. They sit in their state legislatures every year, making laws.

What else can they do? Over the years, the Supreme Court has given the power to prosecuting attorneys and police officers and has taken away freedoms from the people. We are a punitive society, and it shows in our incarceration rate.

WHAT CRIMES DO PEOPLE COMMIT?

Here are the four classifications and the types of crimes committed:

1. **Violent.** Murder, manslaughter, kidnapping, rape, other sexual acts, robbery, and assault.

2. **Property.** Fraud, arson, larceny, theft, stolen property, burglary.

3. **Public Order.** Parole/probation violation, weapons, obstruction of justice, traffic, driving under influence, drunkenness, immigration.

4. **Drugs.** Trafficking, possession, other drug crimes.

The reason why we're all here today is because of a failure of the criminal justice system to properly use probation. So, what happens is these problems are solved by the Legislature because the people in charge … aren't solving the problem."
Senate Judiciary Committee Chairman Tara Nethercott (R-Cheyenne)

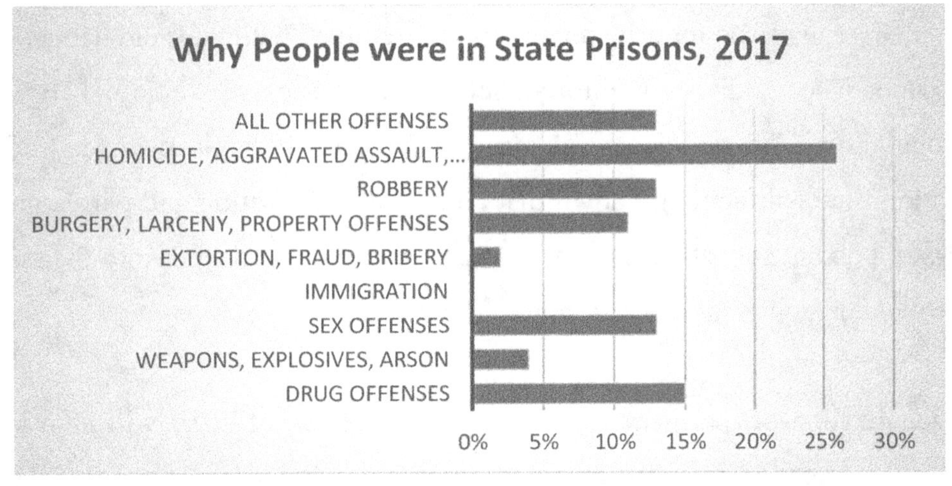

Source: Bronson & Carson. (2019). *Prisoners in 2017.*

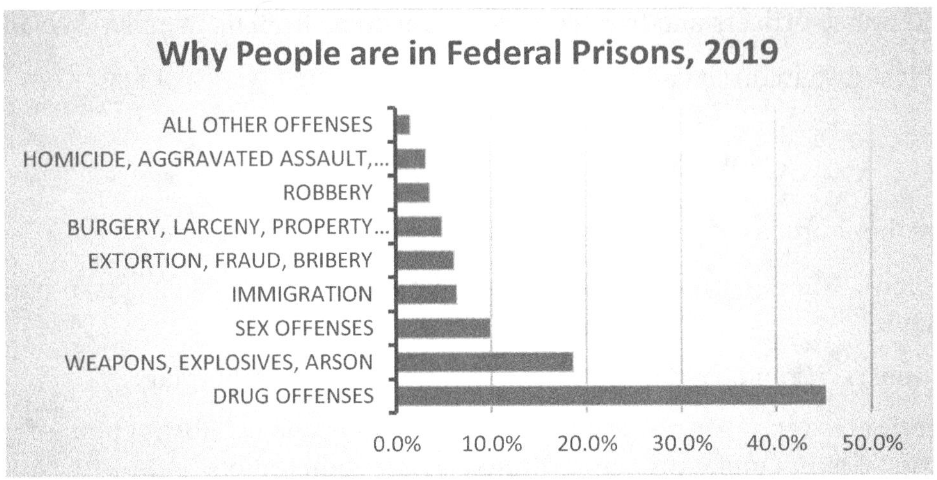

Source: Federal Bureau of Prisons. (2019). *Offenses.*

A FEW FACTS ON DRUG ARRESTS

It takes several years of investigation and an inordinate amount of money to put a serious drug dealer behind bars. While the investigation goes on, the dealer continues to put his goods on the streets and ruins more lives.

Users that go to prison for drug possession are tempted with their old habits; drugs are in prisons, too. The recidivism rate for addiction is high because we do not "rehabilitate" for the long term. To be successful, drug users need lifestyle changes and a grim determination they will never go down that path again. Probation and parole are usually band-aids, and do not solve their need for drugs. As we delve deeper into the subject, we will see drug addiction is merely a symptom of a greater cause.

The legalization of marijuana in thirty-three states as of 2019 will show a drastic decrease in incarceration rates for drugs. According to *Drug War Statistics,* in the year 2017, arrests for possession of marijuana were eighty-five percent of the total drug law violation arrests. Of possession-only charges, ninety percent were marijuana law violations.

Table 4. Comparison of states in the Suicide Belt to suicide, incarceration, violent crime, and correctional control.

2019 RANKINGS FOR STATES IN THE SUICIDE BELT, INCLUDING ALASKA									
Suicide[1]									
MT	AK	WY	NM	ID	UT	CO	NV	OK	AZ
1	2	3	4	5	6	10	11	14	20
World Ranking in Incarceration[2]									
21	26	13	15	20	48	32	17	1	8
Violent Crime Ranking[3]									
26	1	23	2	45	41	24	3	14	12
Correctional Control[4]									
34	31	29	37	3	50	14	44	23	19
Source: [1]Sawyer. (2019). *U.S. States with the highest suicide rates.* [2]Sawyer & Wagner. (20190. *Mass incarceration: The whole pie 2019.* [3]Dillinger. (2019). *The most dangerous states in the U.S.* [4]Jones. (2018). *Correctional control 2018. Incarceration and supervision by state.*									

Black and Latino people comprise most of these arrests (46.9 percent) even though these two groups make up only a third of the total U.S. population.

- White people use five times more drugs than Blacks
- Blacks go to prison ten times more often for drugs than whites
- Time served for Blacks with a drug charge: 58.7 months
- Time served for Whites with a violent crime charge: 61.7 months (Criminal, 2016).

Women get caught up in the legal web with associations with a boyfriend or husband who is in the drug business. Women's arrest rates are rising, and this excerpt from *Overlooked: Women in jails in an era of reform* (2016) offers a great perspective on how someone can unintentionally end up with a drug charge.

> When women face more complex charges, such as those involving other defendants, their typically peripheral roles put them at a decided disadvantage. For example, if their alleged participation was minor, trivial, impromptu, or

uninformed—such as a carrier or small-scale seller of drugs in a drug conspiracy case—they have less leverage to negotiate a favorable plea deal because they have little information about others' crimes or contacts to trade for a lesser sentence. While some women are co-equal or independent actors in criminal activity, even women with minimal or no involvement or knowledge have been increasingly swept into the justice system as the result of the wide application of certain charges, such as conspiracy and accomplice liability.

Complicity law, for example, recognizes no difference between "major" or "minor" accomplices, and accomplices, if found guilty, are not held to a separate, lesser offense of "aiding and abetting," but are treated like the principal actor in terms of guilt and punishment.

As a result, women and other lower-level participants can face the same sentences as their more significantly involved counterparts, for instance, by simply taking a phone message or allowing a partner or family member to keep items at their home.

The warning is clear. If your son or daughter (or boyfriend) has drugs in your house and is arrested, you run the chance of losing your house and facing accomplice charges. You can be sure your child is not telling you they are selling drugs out of your home, so what a surprise it will be when the police come knocking on your door! Say good-bye to your freedom.

JAILS – THE NEIGHBORHOOD GATEKEEPER

"Jails are where our nation's incarceration problem begins and too often serve as warehouses for those too poor to post bail, nonviolent offenders, or people with mental illness.
Julia Stasch, president of MacArthur Foundation

The 2.3 million people behind prison bars does not reflect the trouble with the high incarceration rates as much as jail admissions. Two-thirds more people are incarcerated in jails than prisons. The time served in jails is a year or less, so more people churn through the system.

The greatest number of people are there for one reason: They are too poor (Kilgore, 2015). Their poverty makes them vulnerable to legal trouble. The services that could be helping, like family services, healthcare, and mental-health counseling, are declining, or discontinued altogether.

WHY PEOPLE ARE IN JAIL

Most people are in jail because they are awaiting trial and cannot afford bail, they fail to make their probation appointments, or they cannot pay their fines. Two-thirds of the people in jails are not convicted but waiting for a jury trial.

When people are incarcerated who are not proven to be guilty of the crime, they suffer the same consequences as those who plead guilty. It does not matter what the outcome, an entanglement with the law is an entanglement the public does not want to deal with. If you have legal problems, forget having a life of "liberty and justice."

Failure to pay a fine can cause a person to lose their driver's license, even though the offense had nothing to with a traffic charge.

- People with traffic offenses spend time in jail if they drive on a suspended license.
- The court will suspend a person's driver's license for not making child support payments.
- People will continue to drive because they need to get to their jobs and take care of the transportation needs of their family members.
- Eventually, they are pulled over and face a charge for driving with a suspended license (Kilgore, 2015).

Laundry days are Tuesday and Friday
Have your bag by the door at lockdown. You will get it
back whenever they feel like giving it to you.
(A sign on a jailhouse wall)

And the truth is, even meaningful bail reform is just the beginning. The real work is asking why we are arresting so many people on low-level offenses in the first place, and why so many of them come from poor black and brown communities.

Prison Policy Initiative

A three-day stay in jail can have devastating effects on a person's well-being. A Prison Policy Initiative study revealed that three days in jail can ruin a person's chances of returning to their place of employment or finding other employment. A three-day stay makes obtaining housing more difficult.

After three days in jail, a previously law-abiding citizen becomes a person who will miss court appointments, and probably will commit another crime (Aiken, 2017). When compared to the accused who are not detained, people who stay in jail awaiting their trial frequently plead guilty and serve longer sentences. Breakdowns in system processes are largely responsible for the large numbers of pre-trial detention (Aiken, 2017).

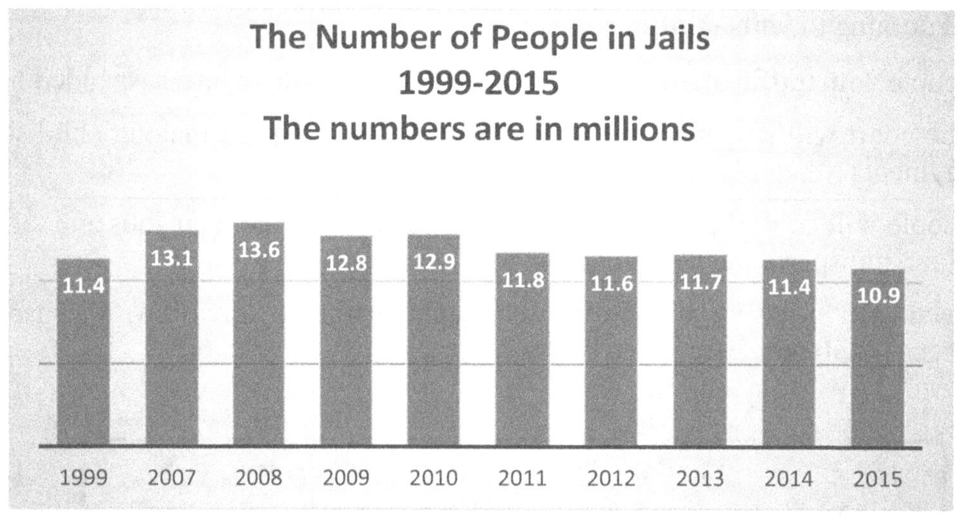

Source: Beck & Harrison. (2001). *Prisoners in 2000.*

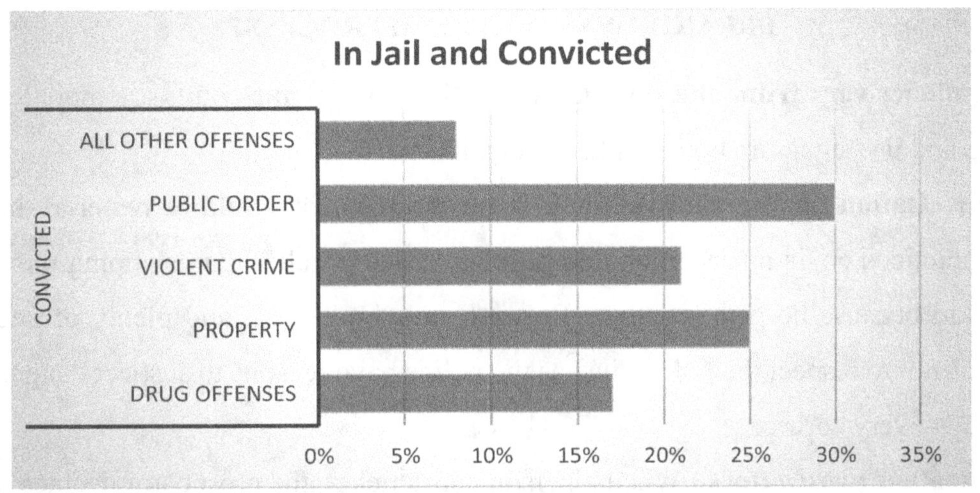

Source: Zeng. (2019). *Jail inmates in 2017.*

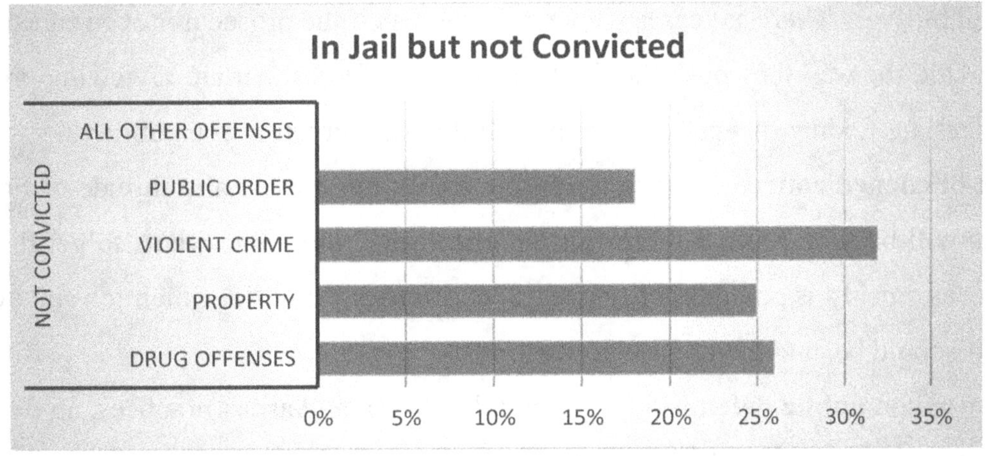

Source: Zeng. (2019). *Jail inmates in 2017.*

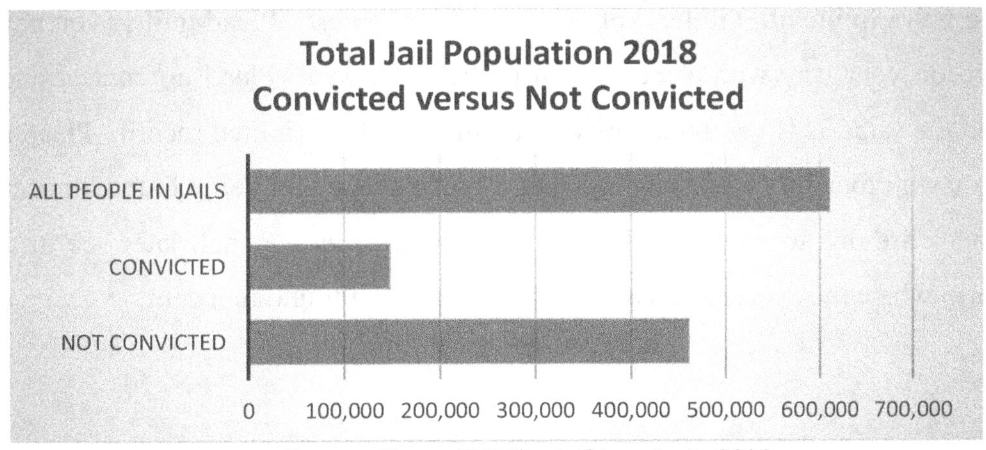

Source: Zeng. (2019). *Jail inmates in 2017.*

BREAKDOWNS IN SYSTEM PROCESSES

1. **Bail policies vary from one jurisdiction to the next.** Some courts are more lenient than others and use signature bonds rather than jail time.

2. **Unfair citation and arrest practices.** Law enforcement would be better at their jobs if they practiced crisis intervention and problem solving rather than slapping the handcuffs on a kid because he gets mouthy. Respect must be earned, and plenty of people have reasons not to respect the police, just as the police have reasons to suspect danger from the public at every corner.

3. **Overzealous prosecutors.** When a person gets a ticket, the prosecutor decides if the case is worth taking to court. A prosecuting attorney is in a powerful position. They have control of lives. There are cases where one wonders if the prosecutor even cares about the defendant, the way they push the limits of the law. States that are reviewing prosecuting practices are finding that prosecutors have little oversight or accountability.

4. **Over-burdened courts.** It goes to reason if the police write a multitude of tickets, the courts will be full. With a room full of "criminals," the judge wants to get through the docket as quickly as possible. He assumes the attorneys have done their job and everything is as it should be, and the process is working.

5. **Overworked public defenders.** With unfair citation and arrest practices, an overzealous prosecutor, and over-burdened courts, the defendant does not have much of a chance in getting a public defender that is not over-worked and who is able to speak well for them.

6. **Three ways to plead.** Guilty, not guilty, and no contest. Plead guilty, you pay the fine and go on your way with a record you probably earned. Plead no contest and you are treated the same as if you pled guilty – complete with a criminal record. Plead not guilty and you wait for a jury trial, with less than a 50/50 chance for being found innocent. These low odds are due to human and political influences, as we shall later see in a real-life scenario where the accused has a zero chance of being found innocent.

7. **Harsh criminalization law.** It is too easy to end up in court. We are inundated with laws, and most of the time we do not even know we are breaking one. It is also too easy to get caught crosswise, especially if you are poor and cannot afford to pay an attorney. Money talks, and if you do not have the money, you do not walk.

8. **Rare or underfunded pretrial services and diversion programs**. Jail should be the last resort when people come before a judge (Aiken, 2017).

The mentally ill end up in jail too frequently. This is not to say the Hannibal Lectors and criminally insane should be allowed on the streets, but with early detection and treatment, we could potentially prevent a horrendous crime from being committed.

An encounter with the law may be the first wave of contact for a person to receive services. Mothers with young children might only need a boost up in life, instead of being put down further because she "allegedly" crossed the line.

Now we are getting to the crux of the matter. Consider the consequences of our punitive actions in incarcerating so many of our citizens. Lawmakers and enforcers, and those who see how unjust our "justice" system is, must take up the gauntlet for reform in the way we deal with our citizens. Chances are you know someone caught up in this iron curtain called justice, or perhaps you have experienced the unfairness of the law yourself.

CRUMBLING JUSTICE

If every state were a country, Wyoming ranks #13 in the world for incarceration. Wyoming is also #2 in the world for incarcerating women.

Do high incarceration rates for women in the Equality State have anything to do with the state's high suicide rates?

In an upcoming chapter, we discuss the plight of many women in America - either living in poverty, having a criminal record, or both.

Single moms raise nineteen million children. Eight out of ten incarcerated women are mothers, the majority with children under 5 years of age.

Wyoming women are no different than any other woman in the U.S. They are not a threat to public safety. While in prison, they are subjected to disciplinary action with steep sanctions that cause them to lose time served and forces them into a longer stay.

Wyoming does not have a woman's boot camp – where men can be out of jail in six months to a year for their crime, women are facing much longer sentences. The children suffer, and women are at risk for losing their parental rights because of long prison terms.

> **5,400 people are locked up in Wyoming's jails and prisons**
>
> 1900 in jail
> 2500 in state prison
> 790 in federal prisons
> 180 in juvenile detention
> 30 in Indian Country
> 30 in involuntary confinement
>
> Wyoming Profile. Prison Policy Initiative

Unfair prosecutorial practices also put women in jails when they do not belong. One woman is taking the rap for her boyfriend who is distributing meth. I say, "is," because as she pays her eighteen months in prison for his freedom, he is out on probation and still up to his old ways. When asked why she took the sentence, she said, "Because I loved him, and I always protect those I love." However, after a few months sitting in jail, waiting for a bed in prison, with nothing to do but sleep, she regrets that decision. The prosecutor should have never let it happen, but then, some prosecutors should not be allowed to practice!

Recent complaints of former inmates in the women's prison at Lusk reveal a prison with a broken heating system, falling ceiling tiles, leaking water pipes, and overcrowding. Women are held in jails after sentenced to prison as they wait for a cell to open, and once there, women are shipped back to jails because of the overcrowding. Threats of sending inmates back to jail are used as discipline.

"If I'm going to have a problem with you, we'll just go ahead and send you to county jail, and you can come back in six months and see if things have changed!"
Graham. (2009). *Woman's prison conditions like 'stockyard' say former inmates.*

One woman complained that when she was sent to the county jail, she was put in a cell that was designated for inmates at-risk for suicide. The camera, monitored by male jailers, gave her no privacy for using the toilet or getting dressed. "When we were going pee, yeah, we were being watched" (Graham, 2009).

While in prison, women can pursue their education and job training. There are resources for rehabilitation in prisons, but in jails, all you do is sit. Meant for short-timers, jails are not set up to house inmates for any length of time.

The men's prison in Rawlins is likewise declining – sinking ground is causing the buildings to shift.

> **"Our punishment is prison. Not to be treated like we're less than nothing, to be treated like we're animals."**
>
> Graham. (2009). *Woman's prison conditions like 'stockyard' say former inmates.*

THE PRISON SYSTEM

A state with a copious number of laws, vigorous pretrial and bail conditions, maximum penalties supported by prosecuting attorneys, and law enforcement over-interpreting their duties, puts 1:130 people in Wyoming in prison or jail and 1:58 residents on probation or parole (Jones, 2018).

Over $300 million is spent annually on Wyoming's corrections system. The cost for each inmate is between $35,000 and $52,000 a year (Horvath & Frost, 2014). This is over twice to three-times more than what a single mother in poverty makes in a year!

While ninety percent of the crimes committed are property crimes, sixty percent of the crimes are marijuana-possession related. Wyomingites are such horrible people, are they not? Destroying property and smoking pot while doing it!

In 2018, the legislature made all laws conform to the same sentencing. A misdemeanor, with property damage of less than $1,000, carries either six months in jail and a $750 fine, or one year in jail and $1,000 fine. Maximum sentences for felonies are five or ten years, with fines of $5,000 to $10,000 for property damage over $1,000.

Some of the laws with jail penalties are defrauding an innkeeper (leaving without paying the bill), stealing motor vehicle fuel, making a shield intended to hide merchandise from an electronic or magnetic theft alarm sensor. True to the Wild West, it is still illegal to rustle (steal) livestock! The relevance of this law will be revealed as we dig into a bit of Wyoming history in Part 4.

Without laws, society runs rampant, but too many laws cause anarchy. A certain group of people are of the criminal mind, but for the most part, people are honest citizens wanting to get through their day without drama or stress. It is probably necessary to have all these laws, just in case someone decides to siphon off and steal gas from a car, for instance, but is it necessary to throw someone in jail for such a small crime?

We have reached the point of diminishing returns with our judicial system. **The $300 million we spend on keeping "criminals" under lock and key could be used in other areas, such as healthcare, education, mental health, and helping children.** Serving jail time destabilizes communities and neighborhoods. In many cases, children who have a parent who was/is incarcerated have legal and mental health issues, use drugs, drop-out of school, and obtain inadequate or nonexistent employment. Is this the fate we want for future generations? With the Wyoming judicial system incarcerating a large portion of her women, the mothers and caretakers of children, we are setting the scene for continued poverty, incarceration, and suicide.

> *"Putting people in prison for victimless crimes is something we shouldn't be doing. It's ruining a lot of people."*
>
> *Bunky Loucks, R-Casper*

There are a few things the Wyoming legislature could do to liberate the citizens of Wyoming from the iron bars. With 1:58 citizens under correctional control, the situation can no longer be ignored. For whatever reason our justice system has gotten to this point, immediate reform is imperative. We can start with such things as:

Deferred and expunged sentences. It is difficult to "forget the past," when the past will not forget you. How can anyone get on with their lives when they keep meeting roadblocks directly related to a mistake they made in younger years, and paid the price?

"Do the crime, do the time." And then some. It is impossible to get the monkey off your back. A misdemeanor is just as damaging as a felony and should be treated with equal regard. Recidivism is because of repeat offenses – if there is no record of a previous crime, there is no recidivism. Society should be protected from the violent criminals, but most people would not be repeat offenders if they were given a chance. A citation is a death sentence for most people, as we have seen, and the punishment far outlives the crime!

Statewide jail reform with yearly inspections and quality control standards. At the present, there is no accountability for jailers, and there are no quality standards for jails. Why do people just sit when they are in jail? Why are they refused medications? Each jail is left to the discretion of those in charge, to the whims of whoever is elected that year.

State-wide officer training in recognizing and controlling the symptoms of trauma, in both themselves and their suspect in the heat of the moment. People are afraid of the police; the police are afraid of people. The "protect and serve" motto no longer serves its purpose. With vigorous training in conflict management, listening skills, and ethics, and arresting people only as the last resort, perhaps respect between civilian and law enforcement could be restored. The officer is the man with the key. He writes the ticket. He is the one that sets the stage for the rest of your life. It is not his job to write the ticket and let the "judge sort it out." His job is to keep the peace and settle disputes – a peacemaker so both parties go home happy. If all officers had a concrete understanding of the interpretation of the law, innocent people would not get caught up in a drama they had no part in.

Boot camp for women. When a man goes to bootcamp, his sentence is shortened. They can get home to their families and a job and get on with their life. Women should be given the same opportunity.

Legalize or decriminalize marijuana. We are leaving money on the table by not legalizing marijuana. Although it is legal to grow hemp, the regulations are strict and prohibit a regular citizen to grow the plant. This is a profitable business, because there are many uses for the marijuana plant, like making paper, clothes, and other necessities. In other states, these proceeds are used to improve healthcare, education, mental health, and services for children. \

Save incarceration for the violent offenders, those who deserve to be there. To know where to re-budget the money that is saved from ending the senseless incarcerations of so many people, first we must know the best places to spend it.

In Part 2, we identify major challenges in housing and employment that at least one-third of America's families contend with daily; and how these challenges configure into the scenario of suicide, incarceration, and poverty.

To do this, five states are chosen from the suicide belt, (Montana, Alaska, Wyoming, New Mexico, and Colorado), with Minnesota and Louisiana as comparison. We are using Minnesota because it is rural and has many of the same demographics as the Mountain States. Louisiana ranks next to New Mexico in many areas, has a large minority population, and competes with the Western states for the worst healthcare.

The data is presented in such a way so you can decipher for yourself the elements that contribute to poverty, suicide, and incarceration. The information stacks upon itself, and the goal is that by the end of the next section, you will have a clear understanding of how the citizens of these states are faring.

Each year, the Annie E. Casey Foundation conducts a Kid Count to determine child well-being in the states and classifies them into the four categories shown in Table 5.

1. Family and Community – neighborhood violence and crime, lack of positive relationships among residents, unhealthy views of drugs and alcohol.

2. Economy – poor economic growth and stability, unemployment, the homeless, poverty. Housing is included here because resident instability, crowded housing, and severe housing conditions have a direct effect on the economy.

3. Education – necessary for rising out of poverty, and the importance of early childhood education.

4. Healthcare - – availability of healthcare, physician shortage, the uninsured. Mental health services are presented in a separate chapter because of the relationship between mental illness, incarceration, poverty, and suicide.

Table 5. Overall rankings of the states.

2019 OVERALL WELL-BEING AND DEMOGRAPHICS OF THE STATES							
		States in the Suicide Belt					
	MN	MT	AK	WY	NM	CO	LA
Overall Child Well-Being[1]	4	22	45	21	50	20	49
Educational Well-Being[1]	10	20	49	14	50	19	48
Economic Well-Being[1]	3	19	33	14	49	12	50
Family & Community Well-Being[1]	8	11	21	9	50	17	48
Health Well-Being[1]	6	44	50	49	48	41	42
Population[3]	5.6 M	1 M	739,000	583,000	2.1 M	327 M	4.6 M
People per square mile[3]	66.6	6.8	1.2	5.8	17	87.4	104.9
Median Age[3]	37.9	40	34.5	37.5	37.7	36.8	36.8
Suicide Rank[4]	38	1	2	3	4	10	29

Source: [1]Kids Count Data Center (2019)
[2]USA Health Ratings (2018)
[3]U.S. Census Bureau
[4]Sawyer. (2019). *U.S. States with the highest suicide rates.*

Part II

THE STATE OF THE NATION

We are trapped in a vicious cycle of economic, intellectual, social, and political death. Inferior jobs, inferior housing, inferior education, which in turn leads to inferior jobs. We spend a lifetime in this vicious circle…giving birth to children who see no hope or future but to follow in our miserable footsteps.

Malcolm X
California, October 11, 1963

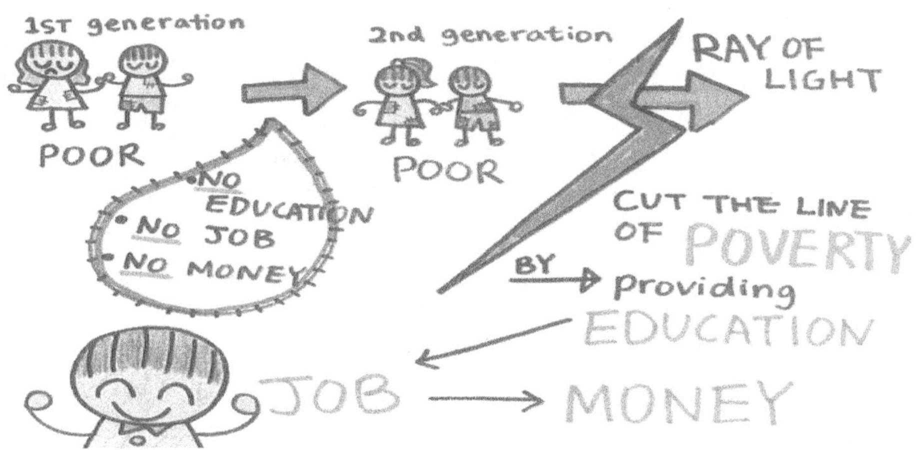

Chapter 3

FAMILY AND COMMUNITY WELL-BEING

Here we are at the heart of belongingness. If families cannot get along, if the community is disorganized, and the neighbors fight among themselves, then children do not experience a necessary tool for survival – belonging to a group. Isolation is a precursor for suicide, and if a child does not make connections at a young age, she tends to always be a loner. There are reasons for this self-inflicted isolation. A child cannot grow up in a home rampant with upheavals and instability and be expected to function well among others. Shields are raised, mistrust is formed, and she learns to fend for herself in a crazy world.

Child maltreatment takes on various forms. We pair child abuse with domestic violence, but negative traits in the community also contribute to childhood violence. Housing cost burden, vacant housing, lack of education, poverty, and unemployment shape children and families. Parents under stress from coping with inadequate living conditions and the other stressors of life become negligent in their parenting, whether intentionally or not. Nearly half of America's children are without the biological father in the home. The family structure has gone by the wayside. The families that do stay intact are often riddled with social, legal, and financial difficulties.

As you continue this journey of life behind the iron curtain, you will begin to see reasons, besides family discord, that have dwindled our society into the state it is today.

A family that plays together stays together. Physical activity is not just for sound mental and physical health but gives a family something to do together that is fun. A weekend away from daily stressors makes life more bearable. Parents who teach their kids healthy ways to wind down are teaching them a valuable lesson in self-care when they become adults.

Believe it or not, children follow what their parents teach, but parents forget they are the #1 model for their children. This is especially true in a home fraught with financial difficulties, poor housing conditions, and probable legal trouble. Parenting is difficult enough without also living in an unstable environment.

Resident turnover. A community with high turnover rate does not have the social cohesion and social support necessary for raising healthy children. When residents move in and out of a community at a fast rate, there is little chance for establishing programs such as parenting programs, stable healthcare, and social support services. Long-term residents are needed for the stability that provides healthcare, good schools, and community programs. Without this vested interest, families suffer and child maltreatment ensues.

Adult-to-child ratio and people 65 and over. This is related to the availability of other adults to help with childcare. Outside of daycare, it is difficult to find family, friends, and neighbors to help supervise children, even for a few hours. The higher ratio of children to adults places a strain on economic and psychological well-being of both family and community.

SINGLE MOTHERS

We know how difficult it is to raise children on your own, plenty of us have experienced it ourselves. It makes no difference whether single mother or single father, the job is a tough one. Raising children is hard enough when two people are involved, but the hard times are double when only one parent is in charge.

Single mothers rank FIRST for living in poverty.

Single parent families are the norm in today's society. In 1960, there were 5 million children in single-parent families, in 2018, there were 19 million.

Poverty Rate among Recent Single Mothers: 44.3%
Total Population of Recent Single Mothers in Poverty: 592,588

Sauter (2018). *Faces of Poverty*

Nearly all single mothers today are welfare recipients. Considering the poverty level, the lack of parental supervision, and unstable housing, it is no wonder that teens who come from homes with a single mother have problems.

This is what a single-parent household looks like, according to a report by the Commission on Peace Officer Standards and Training (Ahlberg):

- 19 million children in the United States are raised by single mothers.
- Mothers are usually in their 20s and have annual incomes of less than $10,000.
- 25 million children have no father at home.
- A little less than half of all live births are born to single moms.
- It is common for children in the same family to have different fathers.

Teens from single-parent families also experience a higher risk of being a gang member, a high school dropout, or attempting suicide. Teen girls are at a high risk for pregnancy, and with this can come substance abuse and homelessness (Ahlberg).

While nearly half of single women with children live in poverty, only eleven percent of mothers who are married live in poverty. Women of low income have unwanted pregnancies five times more frequently than women with higher incomes.

A single parent has a greater difficulty with child supervision, social and instrumental supports are limited, and the parent has challenges of her own (stress and depression), all of which increase the likelihood of child maltreatment (Community, 2019). Indeed, when you tally up the toll on children of single parents, their sacrifice is huge!

Service Workers rank Eleventh for living in poverty.

The next time you are tired and hungry and want a nice meal at a restaurant, think of how the waitress you love so much is part of two-thirds of the work force earning minimum wage ($7.25/hour) or less.

Poverty Rate among Service Workers: 10.7%
Total Population of Service Workers in poverty: 26.2 Million

Sauter (2018). *Faces of Poverty*

Laws are written so that most wait staff make a low hourly wage ($3/hour) and declare their tips. An excellent waitress can make good tip money, and that is what sustains her. If she works for minimum wage, she yields a gross paycheck of $1160 a month.

Is the single-parent family the root cause of our suicide/incarceration/poverty conundrum? With a twenty-five percent increase of single parents since the 1960's; the increasing rates of incarcerating women; and half of America's women in living poverty; one cannot help but wonder if our women are being singled out – a minority of their own.

If you are a single mother, a service worker and have a child under five, your chances for living in poverty are four times higher than a mother who is married. If you are of a minority or have a disability, your chances for poverty increase even more.

Table 6 shows most states do well with family and community as they relate to physical activity, but there is a high resident turnover, and lack of available adults able to help care for children.   The lack of prenatal care and low birth-weight babies is connected to single parent families and parents not employed. Not having adequate prenatal care puts infants at high risk for problems with developmental delays and chronic medical problems.

Table 6. Family and Community as they relate to physical activity, resident turnover, and available adults able to help care for children.

2019 FAMILY AND COMMUNITY WELL-BEING							
		States in the Suicide Belt					
	MN	MT	AK	WY	NM	CO	LA
Family & Community[1]	5	10	20	7	49	17	48
Physical Inactivity[2]	19%	20%	27%	23%	18%	14%	29%
Access to Exercise[2]	87%	75%	n/a	76%	77%	91%	75%
Resident Turnover[3]	14%	16%	19%	18%	14%	19%	13%
Child-Adult ratio[3]	1:3	9:28	7:20	9:26	6:17	8:25	11:3
Age 65 and over[3]	15%	17%	10%	14%	14%	13%	14%
1-parent family[1]	28%	28%	29%	28%	42%	28%	44%
Single Mothers[2]	9%	8%	10%	8%	17%	9%	14%
Parents not Employed[1]	4%	26%	2%	5%	36%	23%	35%
Teen Births per 100,000[1]	13	24	22	26	30	18	31
Low Birth Weight Babies[2]	7%	8%	7%	7%	9%	9%	10.6%
Source: [1]Kids Count Data Book, 2019 [2]County Health Rankings, 2018 [3]Community Opportunity Map							

Chapter 4

ECONOMIC WELL-BEING

Here is where we talk about conditions that foster child maltreatment. When parents are stressed financially, they become absent in their parenting. Few employable skills, growing up in poverty, not having a high-school education, along with criminal charges, are a few reasons why people stay in poverty. Plus, criminality plays a role in unemployment. (Or is it unemployment plays a role in criminality?)

> **2019 U.S. Facts**
> Median income $57,652.
> Unemployment rate 4%
> Poverty rate 12%
> Children in poverty 18%
>
> U.S. Census Bureau QuickFacts

Not only are the unemployed at higher risk for incarceration, but they are also at higher risk for suicide. Although income status does not seem to be related to suicidal tendencies, the unemployed experience a great deal of financial stress.

Adding to the confusion, alcohol consumption and marital discord naturally follows.

Adults who are unemployed rank second for living in poverty.

Poverty causes economic distress, not just for the individual and family, but for the community, as well. Not only are there lost dollars from not working, but there are the added costs of supporting that non-working individual. For instance, unemployed people cannot afford medical care, and use the emergency rooms as their doctor, which puts a cost and resource overload on the healthcare system. When people living in poverty are clustered together, neighborhoods become unstable and disorganized, conflict arises among the residents, law enforcement is called, and someone goes to jail!

Table 7. Comparison of income, unemployment, and poverty of the states.

2019 ECONOMIC WELL-BEING							
		States in the Suicide Belt					
	MN	MT	AK	WY	NM	CO	LA
Economic Well-Being[1]	3	19	33	14	49	12	50
Average Income[2]	$65,699	$43,872	$50,802	$53,302	$46,744	$56,456	$43,445
Unemployment[3]	3.5%	8%	8%	5%	6.2%	5%	7%
Poverty Rate Overall[2]	9.5%	14%	10%	11%	21%	12%	28%
Children in Poverty[3]	12%	16%	15%	13%	26%	12%	28%

Source: [1]Kids Count Data Book, 2019
[2]U.S. Census Bureau
[3]County Health Rankings 2018

Poverty Rate among the unemployed: 30.4%
Total Population of unemployed in poverty: 2.6 million

Sauter, 2018. *Faces of Poverty*

HOUSING COST BURDEN

Ten percent of children live in houses that cost more than fifty percent of their parent's income.
Kids Count Data Book, 2019

When you wake up every morning and the first thing you see are stains on the ceiling, you know your life has taken a turn for the worst. A safe and pleasant shelter is a necessity for sound mental and physical health.

Housing cost burden is present when thirty percent or more of income goes to mortgage or rent and is related to economic distress, housing instability, and food insecurity (Community, 2019). If you are struggling to meet the rent, you are surely struggling to put food on the table and shoes on your kids.

According to the U.S. Census Bureau, the average rent for the seven states we are examining is $900, but the internet and newspapers show much higher housing costs.

> ***To rent a place for $900 with a <u>fifty-percent</u> housing cost burden, the wage earner needs to make $2064 a month before taxes. This translates to a wage of $12.90 an hour.***

The average income for a woman involved in the justice system is $11,700 a year, or $975 a month, or $6 an hour. You do not have to be a math whiz to quickly calculate how far that paycheck will go!

Severe housing problems are issues with the health and safety of the house. Safe plumbing and wiring, adequate kitchen appliances, a roof that does not leak, windows that seal out the cold, walls clean and painted, free of pests and rodents. Safe and pleasant housing is important for a stress-free, mentally healthy life.

Vacant housing in the neighborhood is related to inadequate support and social cohesion between neighbors, and neighborhood deterioration (Community). Businesses are not interested in coming to a community with too many vacant houses, especially in rural areas.

> ***Across the country, every 10% increase in the share of households that are severely cost burdened is linked to 29,000 more children in poverty, 86,000 more people who are food insecure, 84,000 more people in fair or poor health.***
> County Health Rankings, 2018

Between not knowing if there is food for the next meal, when the family will move again, and the stress of the parent, the child learns to fend for herself, which puts her at high risk for youth violence, difficulties in school, and trouble with the law.

Table 8. Correlation of housing cost burden to children living with a high housing cost burden compared to the cost of shelter.

2019 HOUSING WELL-BEING							
		States in the Suicide Belt					
	MN	MT	AK	WY	NM	CO	LA
Vacant Housing[1]	11%	16%	20%	16%	17%	10%	14%
Housing cost burden (HCB)[2]	27%	28%	29%	24%	29%	32%	28%
Severe Housing problems[2]	14%	15%	21%	12%	16%	17%	51%
Low-income children living with HCB[1]	58%	45%	n/a	n/a	48%	67%	55%
Median Gross Rent[3]	$906	$751	$1,200	$828	$809	$982	$825
Median Mortgage[3]	$1,506	$1,344	$1,862	$1,389	$1,244	$1,515	$1,234

Source: [1]Community Opportunity Map
[2]County Health Rankings, 2018
[3]U.S. Census Bureau

INCARCERATING THE HOMELESS

When someone is discharged from jail, they have the possessions they went in with - the clothes on their backs, an empty wallet - and nowhere to go. Some people have family or friends waiting for them, but what about those who do not? What do they do?

Family frequently disowns the incarcerated. When released from prison or jail, inmates have lost all semblance of "normal" to go home to. They have no place to go but to the homeless shelter (or the street). With a few exceptions, the corrections system does not help with this matter, and gives the newly released inmate the meager possessions they brought in with them, heartlessly not providing a coat, clothing, or food.

The ex-prisoner is expected to immediately adjust to a world that is totally different from the one he just came from. Without transportation, but as part of parole, he must find a place to stay, and a job – all within the first 24 hours of release back into society.

What a shock entering the society you left ten or twenty years ago! Everything has changed. Like Rip Van Winkle waking up from a 20-year sleep, the world is completely different. What do you do now?

No wonder the recidivism rate is so high – not only are the previously incarcerated ripe for targeting by law enforcement, which sends them back to prison or jail, but the released inmate will give up his freedom to get back to "three squares and a cot."

There are things worse than imprisonment, especially when that has become your way of life, and you are homeless. The cycle of incarceration/release is repeatedly found in the homeless. A person who is incarcerated within two years or less is twice as likely to be homeless as someone who has not been incarcerated for four years or more (Couloute, 2017).

Police arrest homeless people for infractions that are not common to the rest of the population, such as panhandling or sleeping in public places. Into jail they go for a day or two, back out on the streets with no supports in place, they panhandle and sleep on a public bench, again, and back to jail.

The three largest groups of the homeless are those incarcerated more than once; those incarcerated who are recently released; and people of color (Couloute, 2018). The face of the homeless has changed in recent years. Adding to the normal population of homeless veterans, the mentally ill, and those down on their luck, there is a growing population of younger people. They either live on the streets (unsheltered), on a friend's couch or other fixed residence (sheltered), or in a motel or hotel room (marginal.)

Young people between the ages 18-24, in their transition from home to independence, LGBTQ individuals, and ethnic minorities represent about a tenth of the homeless population. These groups also have an eight-times higher risk for suicide.

- Suicide rates among the homeless are nine times more than the national average.
- Homeless rates for sexual minorities are nearly double that of their heterosexual peers because of social and family conflict concerning their sexuality.
- Individuals with multiple minority identities (e.g., ethnic and LGBTQ) have higher suicide rates than those with single minority status (Holleran & Poon).

Employment and housing laws are geared toward discrimination of the formerly incarcerated. The laws are written in such a way that landowners and housing authorities can screen applicants and not rent to them because of their background. Criminal record checks allow people to punish people for a crime long after it is over. Employment and housing. Two basic needs cannot be met because a person had a run-in with the law.

Along with the criminal record checks to rent a house, comes a credit check, high security deposits, and a professional reference. When a person does not have an address, they cannot get access to healthcare and necessary addiction and mental health services; without an address, they cannot get a job, apply for food stamps, or enroll in educational programs.

An estimated 550,000 people are homeless on any given night in America.

22% are children

69% are over 24

9% are between 18 and 24

60% are male

30% are female

1% are transgender

(Henry et al, 2016)

Chapter 5

EDUCATION WELL-BEING

Students come from all over the world to study in America's world-class universities. With few exceptions, no other place in the world offers quality education and innovative research like American campuses. With this standard of excellence in our upper education, one would think we would be preparing our school-age students for success in our own top-rated universities.

However, you will find that is not the case. In the United States, two-thirds of fourth graders are not proficient in reading, and two-thirds of eighth graders are not proficient in math (Kids, 2019).

> ***Half of the children that start out at the lowest one-fifth of the income level stay there. Forty-five percent of those with a less-than high-school education stay in the bottom one-fifth of the income level.***
> Kids Count Data Book, 2019

With limited education comes low quality employment and the lowest wages on the income scale. Parents lacking adequate education have more unplanned pregnancies.

Lower educated people have inadequate social support, and depend on food stamps, cash welfare payments, and the limited services their community offers. And, what a surprise – those with little education are most likely to be incarcerated!

Two thirds of children in fourth and eighth grades are not proficient in math or reading, but all but a fifth of this population make a speedy recovery and graduate from high school. Is this the fifth that stays on the bottom of the income ladder? The fifth who will never rise out of poverty? Children who attend preschool do better in the earlier grades than those who do not. By the time the child reaches third grade, if they are not catching on, they begin the backslide, and are ripe for trouble (Kids, 2019).

Adults with less than a high school education rank fifth for living in poverty.

Poverty Rate among Adults with less than a high school education: 24.7%
Total Population of Adults with less than a high school education: 64 million

Sauter, 2018. *Faces of Poverty*

THE IMPORTANCE OF CHILDCARE

Women miss their court appointments and end up in jail because they have no one to watch their children. Daycare paid by the state will only cover working hours. Low-income mothers cannot afford to pay for childcare outside of their job. A woman's probation will be revoked if she cannot make a probation appointment or a court date, and the judge does not care if her noncompliance is due to an absence of childcare.

But the need for childcare is not just for incarcerated women.

A woman who works off hours, such as service workers, has no one to care for her children. The childcare centers operate only during daylight hours, so when a mother works the later shifts, she farms her children out to whoever will watch them. This means relatives, boyfriends, and teenage sitters. Once again, low-income children bear the consequences.

Quality childcare has low staff/child ratios, small group sizes, and low turnover among the staff. The staff is trained in early childhood development. They recognize behavior and developmental concerns and have positive expectations of the children's behavior.

The main goal of the childcare centers is to provide care for the children of working mothers, but just as importantly they must provide a positive learning environment. Quality early learning and care centers are integral to a child's school readiness. The years of birth to five are critically important for a child's brain development in emotional, physical, social, and intellectual growth. The child's willingness to learn is stimulated by their environment. A safe, caring, educational-filled high-quality learning environment in early childhood is essential in ensuring the child's success in school and in life.

Kindergarten teachers report that half of their children cannot follow directions, lack basic academic skills, and are not able to work independently. This is especially troubling since children entering kindergarten must know their numbers and letters, and the connections between letters and sounds. Children who enter kindergarten behind their peers may never catch up (Brown, 2001).

Children who complete preschool programs have an advantage in language and reading skills, creativity, music, movement, and social skills (Brown, 2001). Children who are ready to learn will:

- Score higher on school readiness tests.
- Be better prepared academically, especially in reading and math skills.

A high-quality learning environment in early childhood is essential for the child's success in school and life.   The percentage of children 3 to 4 years old who are not in preschool is consistent with the percentage of 4th and 8th graders not proficient in reading or math.

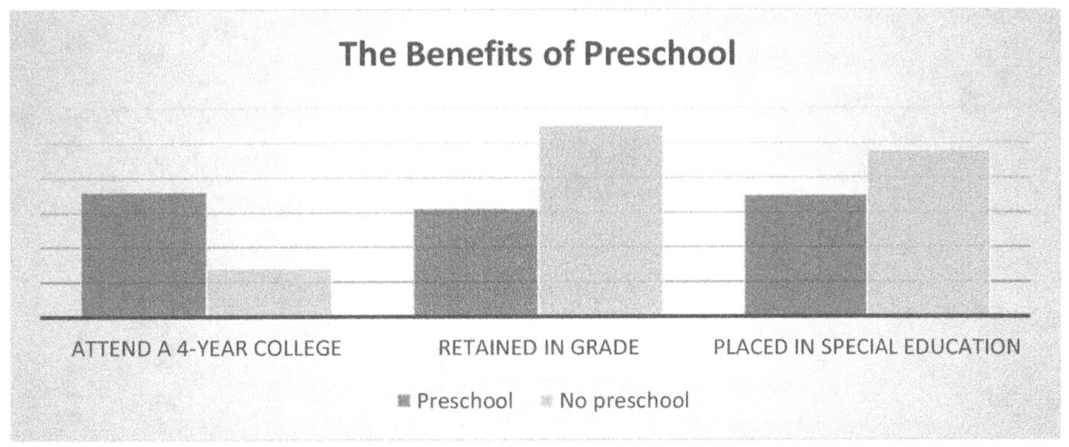

Source: Economic Opportunity Institute

Early childhood education is an excellent return on investment. Long-term benefits of early childhood education are these:

- Higher high school graduation rates
- More than twice as likely to attend a four-year college
- Less chance of requiring remedial education or held back a grade

For every $1 spent on early learning, society saves $7 in later costs.
Economic Opportunity Institute

For schools, for every $1 invested in preschool education, there are reduced costs of $0.73 for remedial and special education (Brown, 2001). The benefits are long-lasting.

Middle school students who received early childhood education have a lower likelihood of entering juvenile detention programs. As adults, they have better chances at high-skilled jobs, are not as inclined to commit a crime or felony, or to rely on social assistance programs (Children's, 2013).

It appears if we want to reduce incarceration rates and poverty, early-childhood education is the answer.

If the wage earner makes $12.90/hour, or $2,064 a month before taxes, and pays $900 a month in rent, plus $600 a month for childcare for one child, this leaves $564 for food, utilities, clothing, and taxes.

Table 9. Correlation between preschool attendance, 4th and 8th grade proficiencies, and teens not graduating from high school.

2019 EDUCATION WELL-BEING OF THE STATES							
		States in the Suicide Belt					
	MN	MT	AK	WY	NM	CO	LA
Educational Well-Being[1]	10	22	49	14	50	19	48
3-4-year-olds not in school[1]	55%	57%	64%	59%	57%	49%	49%
4th graders not proficient in reading[1]	61%	62%	72%	59%	75%	60%	74%
8th graders not proficient in math[2]	54%	62%	71%	62%	75%	62%	81%
High school or GED[1]	83%	86%	92%	93%	71%	91%	80%
Some College[1]	75%	68%	n/a	62%	60%	60%	67%
Not graduated from H.S. on time[1]	18%	5%	24%	20%	29%	21%	21%
Teens not in school, not working[1]	5%	7%	7%	5%	10%	23%	11%
Source: [1]Kids Count Data Center, 2019 [2]County Health Rankings, 2018							

Chapter 6

HEALTH WELL-BEING

A family-care physician who lives in the community and knows the people and their history seems to have gone away with Obamacare. Now hospitals and clinics use physician assistants, rotate their doctors, and use rent-a-docs for emergency care. Today's physician is not interested in the ungodly hours and time away from family that historically came with the job. They seek employment in clinics that offer 40-hour work weeks and a professional staff that assists in taking care of patients, such as physician assistants.

Patients want convenient, reliable, effective treatments by someone they trust and who is empathic to both their physical and environmental concerns. They want the best possible care and expect it to be there when they need it. And they want an advocate that guides them to make the best healthcare choices (Kovner & Knickman, 2008).

What patients need, but many times do not get, is simple instructions for their medications and health behaviors. A normal office visits lasts seventeen minutes, and the patient and physician cover an average of six topics. Five minutes are spent on one topic, and one minute on each of the others (Tai-Seale, 2007). This leaves seven minutes to discuss treatment options, and to confirm the patient understands their medication dosages and any other instructions the doctor might give.

But this is not to blame on the physicians. In response to numerous complaints that primary care physicians were failing to follow evidence-based practices, researchers constructed a model physician practice that matched the U.S. population for age, gender, and prevalence of the ten-most common chronic diseases. The mock practice consisted of 2,500 hypothetical patients. Note that rural practices have more than 2,500 patients, with usually only one or two doctors serving an entire county.

The researchers found that a physician's time was spread thin. Based on real-time estimates, a physician spends three and a half hours a day for the chronically ill whose illness was controlled, and ten-and-a-half-hours for the chronically ill whose disease was not controlled. The remaining seven-and-a-half hours focused on delivering preventive care services. These calculations do not account for the care of acutely ill patients with colds, flu, and injuries. We know doctors put in long hours, but to give the care necessary to every patient in his practice as outlined in the research model, the physician would spend twenty-one-and-a-half hours a day seeing patients (Kovner & Knickman, 2008), with two-thirds of the day caring for chronically ill patients.

High out-of-pocket deductions prevent people with multiple chronic conditions to seek treatment. Untreated diseases eventually put a greater load on healthcare resources because of the extent it takes to treat someone who is severely ill - conditions that in the early stages were treatable, or even preventable.

Although the supply of primary care physicians has remained about the same over the years, the demand is beginning to outperform the supply. Physicians are nearing retirement without enough young doctors to replace them. More women are in the workforce and prefer metropolitan areas over rural, and to work fewer hours so they can meet the needs of their family.

According to the Rural Health Association, the ratio of patient-to-primary-care physicians is 39.8 per 100,000 in rural areas compared to 53.3 per 100,000 in urban areas. This is troubling, because the poorest and those with the most chronic diseases live in rural areas.

THE UNINSURED

Emergency rooms, outpatient clinics, and community health centers must accept a patient even if the only source of payment is self-pay. An emergency room visit is the most expensive and writing off these services affects available operating revenue.

Having insurance or not determines the extent of physical- and mental-health care a person receives. Uninsured people do not receive common diagnostic tests such as colonoscopies and mammograms, or have expensive surgical procedures, such as cardiac bypass and hip replacements.

There are substantial handicaps for people without insurance:

- Uninsured mothers begin prenatal care later and have fewer total visits.
- Uninsured newborns frequently have adverse outcomes.
- Uninsured women present with later stage breast cancer– and run twice the risk of death (Kovner & Knickman, 2008).

Those living in poverty are least likely to have health insurance. The #1 reason is this: They cannot afford the premiums. The average insurance premium in 2017 was $400 for an individual and $1,168 for a family of four. Unless both parents are working full time at $12.90 an hour, there is little room for an emergency or a mistake in spending.

If the wage earner makes $12.90/hour, or $2,064 a month before taxes, and pays $900 a month in rent, $600 a month for childcare for one child, and $1,168 a month for insurance premium, this leaves minus (-) $604 for food, utilities, clothing, and taxes.

It is expensive not to have insurance, especially for the hospitals and emergency rooms that are required to treat people that cannot pay. But it is also expensive for those who cannot afford insurance – they either pay big money out of pocket or wait for treatment until their health has taken a drastic turn for the worst.

The cost to the state would be compensated if people paid premiums based on their income (those with low income do not pay), with the money deposited into a collective fund, and those who need it utilize it.

States that refused Medicaid expansion are seeing the results in hospitals struggling to stay open and people going without healthcare.

Further expanding Medicaid would not solve all the obstacles people face accessing healthcare, but it is a start in the right direction. Operating revenue for hospitals would increase, patients would no longer struggle to pay their medical bills and face bankruptcy.

Table 10. The uninsured and correlation between obesity and poor health days.

2019 HEALTH WELL-BEING OF THE STATES							
		States in the Suicide Belt					
	MN	MT	AK	WY	NM	CO	LA
Health Rankings[1]	6	44	50	49	48	41	42
Obesity[2]	28%	25%	30%	29%	26%	21%	29%
Poor health days[2]	3.0	3.0	3.3	3.2	4.3	2.5	6.0
Uninsured Adults[1]	5%	15%	22%	15%	10%	14%	11%
Uninsured Children[1]	3%	5%	9%	9%	5%	4%	3%
[1] **Source:** Kids Count Data Center, 2019 [2]County Health Rankings, 2019							

Chapter 7

MENTAL HEALTH WELL-BEING

Less than one-half of those needing treatment receive it, but there seems to be no hesitation to incarcerate someone who is mentally ill.

The same concern for medical doctors applies to psychiatrists, but to a larger extent. Over half of the nation's psychiatrists are over 55, getting ready to retire, and fewer medical students are choosing psychiatry as their specialty.

Mental health services are not a priority for hospitals because they prefer expensive procedures that pay profits and show immediate results. Counselling services cover the long term and show little profit. For reimbursement purposes and to counteract the low-profit margin, mental health centers strive for patient volume over value of care to keep their practices viable.

According to the National Alliance on Mental Illness (NAMI):

- 1:5 adults in America have some form of mental illness

- 13.6 million adults live with a serious mental illness (SMI)

- 1:4 adults with a mental illness did not receive mental health services in the previous year

- The average delay between onset of mental health symptoms and intervention is eight to ten years

- Annual lost earnings of $193 billion a year is due to mental illness

- One-third of children needing mental health treatment in 2016 did not receive it

- Half to two-thirds of adults with symptoms of a mental illness did not receive treatment in 2013-2015 (Radly, McCarthy & Hayes, 2018).

The most common mental disorders are depression and other mood disorders, such as schizophrenia, panic attacks, anxiety, and post-traumatic stress. Alzheimer's disease will affect 5.8 million Americans in 2019 and is rapidly increasing in prevalence. There are also the caregivers, who experience mental health issues from the stress of caregiving.

- Nearly one-fourth of the caregivers of people with Alzheimer's and dementia are in the "sandwich generation" – caring for both someone with the disease and a child or grandchild.
- Diagnoses affecting children is on the rise – autism, attention hyperactivity disorder, and post-traumatic stress.
- 1:6 Alzheimer's and dementia caregivers quit their jobs because they become weighted down by their caregiving duties.
- Over half of the caregivers reported high or very high emotional stress.
- Three-quarters of caregivers of people with Alzheimer's disease and other dementias are "somewhat concerned" to "very concerned" about maintaining their own health since becoming a caregiver (Alzheimer's, 2017).

If people could resolve their troubled past, they would not have the struggles they do. There would be fewer people with addictions, domestic violence would decrease, and people in general would be happier and more productive.

Evidence-based trauma therapy can make a remarkable difference in relieving chronic pain. Chronic diseases are unresolved suffering, hidden in the body, begging to be released. As children we learn we are "okay" when we scrape a knee, but as the bruises and bangs become more severe, especially the mental ones, we ignore them as much as we ignore a scrape. This causes problems both mentally and physically.

With simple techniques that can be used outside of counselling, setbacks are lessened, and addictions abate. Generally, after being out of treatment for a year, a person is back to their old ways, but evidence-based trauma therapy has a long-term effect.

Neurofeedback works great for children. Their brains are still forming, and reconnecting or rebuilding disrupted pathways is an easier process than with adults. Some NFB programs are easy to operate; place a few leads on various places on the head and let the program do the work. There can be counselling during the treatment, but NFB is effective with or without a therapist present.

If schools were equipped with NFB, and children were identified before the damaging symptoms manifested into serious misbehaving, we would immediately, and possibly permanently, reduce their risk for addiction, behavior problems, and all that goes with it.

Table 11. Mental health well-being in relation to suicide rates and ranks and poor mental health days.

MENTAL HEALTH WELL-BEING OF THE STATES							
	States in the Suicide Belt						
	MN	MT	AK	WY	NM	CO	LA
Health Rankings[1]	6	44	50	49	48	41	42
Suicide Rank per 100K[1]	38	1	2	3	4	10	29
Range of occurrence of suicides[1]	6.61-21.08	3.45-35.67	6.89 – 70.9	12.95-30.4	13.18-44.86	9.99-39.81	5.74-21.91
Poor mental health days[2]	3.2	3.5	3.4	3.6	4.0	3.5	4.2
Source: [1]Center for Disease Control, Suicide Facts 2018 [2]Kids Count Data Center, 2019							

INCARCERATING AMERICA'S MENTALLY ILL

There is not a single county in the United States where a psychiatric facility holds more people with mental illness than the county jail.
James Kilgore, 2015

According to the National Alliance on Mental Illness (NAMI), an estimated two million people with a mental illness are booked into jails each year (Serious, 2016).

Most of these individuals have not committed violent crimes, have not gone to trial, and are not yet convicted of a crime. Once a person with a mental illness ends up in jail, they begin a decline. They do not receive treatment because jail policies do not allow administration of the medications they are prescribed, and their difficulties escalate.

As one jailer stated, "If they have a meltdown, we just watch them melt."

People with a mental illness who are incarcerated stay longer than their counterparts, and they are at high risk for victimization, from both the jail personnel and cell mates. When they leave jail, they may have lost their access to healthcare benefits.

Like all other incarcerated people, they lose their job, their home, and become homeless. Many end up in the emergency room because of the unstable turn in their life and they can no longer cope.

When someone tries to commit suicide, the protocol is to put them on a 72-hour hold, either in the hospital, or in jail, depending on policies. The judge then determines if they are mentally unstable, and if so, will send them for a 30-day evaluation in the state mental hospital.

Either way, three days in jail or thirty days in involuntary confinement, the consequences are the same. Lost income, mounting bills, eventually they lose their home.

A person with PTSD is not stark-raving crazy, unless unattended to and allowed to deteriorate. People suffering from PTSD hold jobs and manage families. There are a group of psychiatrists and psychologists who believe that placing a diagnosis of "mentally ill" on someone who is traumatized is labeling them inappropriately. We need to rethink the idea of mental illness, both in our expectations of behavior and the way we counsel them. Most mental illnesses have a physical manifestation, and can be managed with medication, diet, sleep, and lack of stress.

People who are traumatized in childhood lead a life dealing with those ordeals. This affects their behaviors, their relationships, and sometimes their freedom. An event that they had no control over, at a young age, has permanently changed their life, and our judicial practices only make things worse. This is how people with a mental illness are treated by the criminal justice system:

Longer length of stay.   They sometimes have difficulty controlling their behavior, cannot follow the rules, and time is added onto their term.

Pretrial waits for psychiatric examinations can be anywhere from thirty-days to a year. Jail inmates wait longer behind bars for their competency evaluation, so they can be tried, than if they were to serve time for the offense for which they are awaiting trial.

Behavior management concerns, especially for those in solitary confinement. A 2010 study of three of Wisconsin prisons reported nearly three-quarters of the inmates in isolation were mentally ill.

> *Suicide is the leading cause of death in correctional facilities. An estimated half of all inmate-suicides are committed by those with a mental illness.*
> Vera Institute of Justice

HEALTHCARE AND MENTAL HEALTH SERVICES IN WYOMING

The Annie E. Casey Foundation's Kids Count ranked Wyoming as #49 in healthcare well-being in 2019. Each of the twenty-three counties has a hospital, but healthcare changes in the last ten years have deeply affected both the residents and the providers.

Hospitals are struggling nationwide to stay in operation with rising healthcare costs, high patient demand, and their obligation to the uninsured. Wyoming has not approved Medicaid expansion, and without it, the few meager programs that were helping people, like mental health services, home health, and assistance for caregivers, were eliminated or downgraded. Lack of supportive services presents a difficult situation for a family member who is the sole provider of a loved one who is chronically ill. In communities with a high disability population, caregivers are extremely stressed, overworked, and unsupported.

With insurance tightening the length of stays in hospitals, patients are discharged before they are ready. In many cases, the patient is released home with no one to care for them afterwards. Family and friends drop in and bring a casserole, but where is the help with wounds and after-surgery care?

Healthcare and mental health services are fragmented, and people find it necessary to travel to one of the major hospitals in states surrounding Wyoming to receive the care they need.

There are not enough medical doctors or psychiatrists to meet the need. In 2016, there were forty-one psychiatrists in Wyoming. Twenty-three were 55 years of age and over and getting ready to retire.

The previous governor appropriated $10 million out of Wyoming's "rainy-day" fund to sponsor a suicide prevention program. Ideally, the best way to spend that money is training groups of people to deliver evidenced-based trauma therapy. Pastors, school counsellors, coaches, nurses, a Sunday School teacher; anyone with a background in listening and empathy can help a person in need. Mental-health first-aid, so to speak.

It does no good to concentrate on serving one group of people (the incarcerated) and not the entire population. By the ripple effect, many people are affected by one incarceration or one suicide, and judging from the high rates, it is safe to say everyone could use a little counselling.

Because of Wyoming's sparse population, it would not be difficult to deliver optimal services to everyone who needed them. Our population would disappear if placed inside one of the large cities in America, and if a city can deliver services to millions of people, we can serve our half-a-million residents. It would take a concerted effort on the part of all concerned. That, in itself, is a challenge.

THE ELEVEN GROUPS MOST LIKELY TO LIVE IN POVERTY

11. Service Workers.
Poverty Rate among Service Workers: 10.7%
Percent of Service Workers that comprise the Poor Population: 6.6%

10. Women.
Poverty Rate among Women: 14.5%
Percent of Women that comprise the Poor Population: 55.4%

9.   Hispanics and Latinos
Poverty Rate among Hispanics and Latinos: 19.4%
Percent of Hispanics and Latinos that comprise the Poor Population: 26.2%

8.   Children under 5.
Poverty Rate among Children under 5: 20.2%
Percent of Children under 5 that comprise the Poor Population: 9.2%

7.   Non-citizen Immigrants.
Poverty Rate among Non-citizen Immigrants: 20.4%
Percent of Non-citizen Immigrants that comprise the Poor Population: 10.6%

6.   Blacks and African Americans.
Poverty Rate among Blacks and African Americans: 23.0%
Percent of Blacks and Americans that comprise the Poor Population: 21.4%

5.   Adults with less than a high school diploma.
Poverty Rate among Adults with less than a high school diploma: 24.7%
Percent of Adults with less than a high school diploma that comprise the Poor Population: 14.9%

4.   American Indian and Alaskan Natives.
Poverty Rate among American Indian and Alaskan Natives: 25.4%
Percent of American Indians and Alaskan Natives that comprise the Poor Population: 1.6%

3.   Americans with a Disability.
Poverty Rate among Americans with a Disability: 25.7%
Percent of Americans with a Disability that comprise the Poor Population: 22.6%

2.   The Unemployed.
Poverty Rate among the Unemployed: 30.4%
Percent of the Unemployed that comprise the Poor Population: 6.1%

1.   Recent Single Mothers.
Poverty Rate among Recent Single Mothers: 44.3%
Percent of Recent Single Mothers that comprise the Poor Population: 1.4%

Sauter. (2018). *Faces of poverty: What racial, social groups are more likely to experience it*

Part III

HAVE FAITH, HOME GIRL, AND LOSE NO HOPE

*We are actually fighting for rights that are even greater than civil rights-
and that is human rights.*

Malcolm X
New York, April 8, 1964

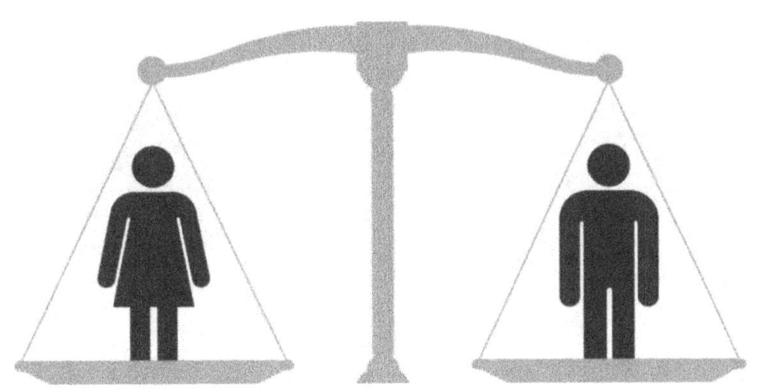

Chapter 8

EQUALITY AND WOMAN'S SUFFRAGE

In 1869, the Wyoming Legislature approved the right for women to vote. Wyoming was the only territory, state, or country in the world that recognized women as political equals. The bill also gave women the freedom to own property. This was provided to protect them from "shiftless and improvident husbands" (Sodaro & Adams, 1996). It was also a move to bring more settlers to the area, especially women. The ratio of men to women was six to one, with a grand total of 1,680 women.

Along with the right to vote, the 1869 legislature agreed that women were allowed in the chambers to watch bills formed in the legislature; teachers would be paid the same whether male or female; and women were guaranteed property rights separate from their husbands (Sodaro & Adams, 1998).

Back when the west was still unsettled and the Indians and buffalo roamed the plains, the life of a pioneer woman was one of little rest. They worked the fields and took care of the livestock right along with their husbands, as well as doing their "womanly" chores. The pioneer women were independent, physically strong, and mentally resilient. They deserved the right to vote and own property. A few women ran their own farms. The first claim filed in Wyoming was by Mrs. Margaret Dolan from Florida, a single woman with six kids (Sodaro & Adams, 1996). Can you imagine, roughing the wilds of Wyoming on your own with six children to feed?

> Yet because of the isolation of Wyoming, barriers between men and women never really existed. A woman, for example, could easily become a widow and be left with a ranch or business to run unaided by any male relatives. On the trail, women's and men's jobs often became indistinguishable. Further, men depended on women not only as homemakers, but as partners (Sodaro & Adams, 1998).

Although the supporters of the bill were dead serious, many of the men in the legislature thought giving the "little woman" the right to vote was a joke.

I remember distinctly a lot of my friends laughing, saying they thought it would be
a good joke to pass the bill.
Ben Sheets, Legislator
(Sodaro & Adams, 1998)

Equal rights became a little sticky in the elections of 1890 when Wyoming became a state. The Republican Congress was against continuing allowing women to vote.

"Giving women the right to vote goes against the very core of
the American Government"
Sodaro & Adams, 1998

But the Wyoming legislature felt continuing woman's suffrage was a good thing for the new state. More settlers would come, and women's suffrage would attract more women. Despite the criticism, Governor John Hoyt was heard to say, "No man has ever dared to say in the territory of Wyoming that woman's suffrage is a failure" (Sodaro & Adams, 1998).

By the time woman's suffrage latched onto the entire country, women in Wyoming were owning businesses and running ranches. Things have certainly changed for the women in the equality state. Having the right to vote and own land, and being treated as an equal,

Isn't it ironic? Wyoming was #1 in the world to grant women the right to vote, but today, she ranks #2 in the world for incarcerating women!

are apparently two different sides of the equality coin. Today, according to the information presented in this chapter, many women in Wyoming are fighting the legal system, instead of running ranches or owning businesses, or raising productive, civic-minded children.

INCARCERATING AMERICA'S MOTHERS

Women often become involved with the justice system as a result of efforts to cope with life challenges such as poverty, unemployment, and significant physical or behavioral health struggles. Most are jailed for low-level, nonviolent offenses. Once incarcerated, women must grapple with systems designed primarily for men. As a result, women leave jail with diminished prospects for physical and behavioral health recovery, as well as greater parental stress and financial instability.
VERA Institute of Justice

Women are trapped in the troubles of legal problems and incarceration at an amazing rate. Caught on the legal hamster wheel, they find it nearly impossible get off. Once targeted as a "criminal," future contact with the law puts them in the forefront. The chances are greater that an officer will arrest someone with a record than someone with no record.

Compliance is especially difficult among women because they are the mothers. Single moms already struggling to make ends meet. One in five children of incarcerated mothers are under 5 years old, and 1.5 million adults under correctional control are parents to 8.3 million children (Facts, 2019).

The annual income for a woman in the system is $11,700. A black woman's average income is $9,000. Bail bonds are usually set at $10,000. An entire year's salary! Even at ten percent nonrefundable bond fee, that is still more than one month's wages. One-half of all Black and Hispanic single moms have a net worth of zero or less (-0) (Facts, 2019). Who has $1,000 laying around for any kind of emergency, let alone an unplanned arrest?

Women rank Tenth for living in poverty.

Poverty Rate among Women: 14.5%
Total Population of Women in poverty: 23.6 Million

Sauter, 2018, *Faces of Poverty*

Women work at more low-paying jobs than men and spend more time in unpaid caregiving of children and elderly family members.

Black women live in poverty and receive public assistance five times more than white women. A stay in jail can cause termination of public assistance, employment, student loans, and housing.

Women in dire poverty cannot afford groceries, let alone daycare. Precarious finances and their predicament with the law lead to a financial crisis that leads to jail – the direct pathway to pay off "onerous criminal debt" (Swavola & Subramanian, 2016).

The number of women in prisons and jails in the United States has never been higher.

Three out of four women in the correctional system are on probation. They are faced with unrealistic expectations that they cannot meet, which cause them to run afoul of the law. Expectations such as:

1. Steep court fees and fines they cannot afford.
2. Not able to post a bail bond.
3. No available childcare for them to make it to their probation appointment.
4. No available or reliable transportation to court dates and probation appointments, especially in rural communities

Costs associated with incarceration and probation are such things as bail; the nonrefundable money paid to the bail bondsman; public defender fees and reimbursement; hundreds of dollars of court costs and fees; electronic monitoring devices; and some states have pay-to-stay programs, charging the inmate for the days they are incarcerated. For instance, California charges $142 a day (Rabuy & Kopf, 2016).

Then there is the high cost of phone calls while in jail. In one jail, a phone card costs $11, the jail keeps $1, leaving $10 for one phone call for less than five minutes.

A comparison of incarceration rates of women in the world and among other states, and the percentage of children with incarcerated parents is found in Table 12 at the end of this chapter, but here are some other startling facts about women and incarceration:

- The 25 jurisdictions with the highest rates of incarcerating women are all American states.
- Thailand, at number 26, is the first non-U.S. government to appear on this list, followed by the United States at number 27.
- The next 17 jurisdictions are also American states.
- Apart from Thailand and the U.S. itself, the top 44 jurisdictions throughout the world with the highest rate of incarcerating women are individual American states (Kajstura & Immarigeon).

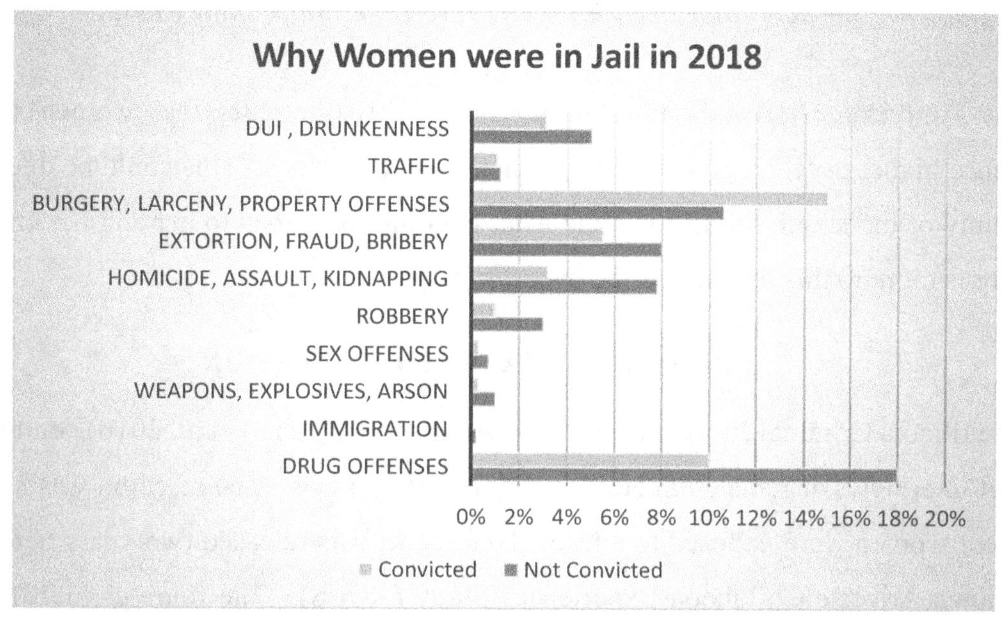

Source: Kajstura & Immarigeon. *States of Women's Incarceration: The global context.*

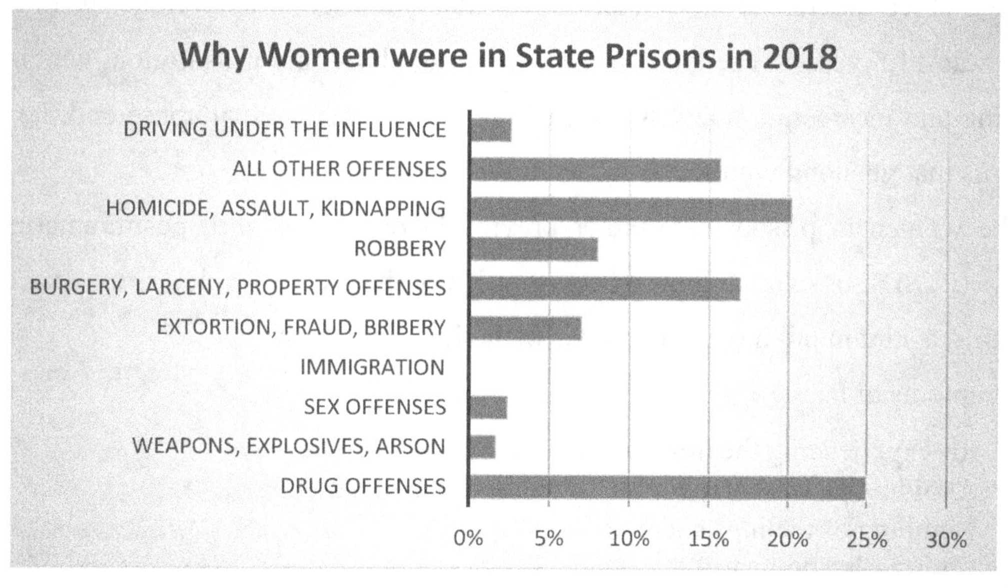

Source: Kajstura & Immarigeon *States of Women's Incarceration: The global context.*

Nearly one-third of the world's incarcerated women are in the United State; twice the percentage of China and four times more than Russia
Prison Policy Initiative

The American Civil Liberties Union (Facts, 2019) reports that women in jails experience higher psychological distress than women in prisons. This could be due to the uncertainty of the length of jail-time and what is going to happen to her and her children, but there is more to this than meets the eye.

CHILD MALTREATMENT IS COMMON

The Illinois Criminal Justice Information Authority (Reichert et al, 2010) conducted a series of interviews of female inmates in Illinois state prisons. The research was to study the extent women were exposed to abuse. This report was released two years before the well-known Adverse Childhood Experiences Study (ACES). The findings in 2010 may have been surprising at the time but was later confirmed by the ACES. The following information is from the Illinois prison study.

Virtually all the women in the study (99%) had experienced some form of abuse as children. Three-quarters of the women were sexually abused, - the average age of the first assault was 11.5 years. The women felt their drug abuse and prostitution, which led to offending and incarceration and was clearly related to their sexual abuse and the victim behaviors that go along with it.

The women in prison were either previously diagnosed with posttraumatic stress disorder (PTSD), or exhibited the symptoms, if not diagnosed. Since stress exacerbates symptoms, a stint in jail most likely made their situation worse.

Symptoms of PTSD:

- Re-experiencing the trauma over and over in various ways
- Avoiding places and people that trigger symptoms
- Numbing of feelings and emotions
- Constantly "on guard"
- Impaired daily functioning
- Difficulty with relationships
- Difficulty keeping employment

Sexual abuse victims are especially at risk for lifetime psychiatric disorders such as borderline personality disorder. They experience turbulent social and interpersonal relationships and have a high potential for revictimization, sexual assault, and partner violence. Plus, there is the potential for high-risk sexual behavior with multiple sex partners, unwanted pregnancies, trading sex for drugs, and prostitution.

Is incarceration the best solution for a woman who is fragile from abuse?

The criminal system is based on crimes committed by males. Even though the incarceration rates for women are rising, they are a small proportion (<10%) when compared to male inmates. Sentencing laws are based on male characteristics and crimes, and do not consider women's roles and experiences.

Often, the courts are a young woman's first contact with the system. What more of a perfect opportunity to sift out women who cannot cope with their past abuse. Offer therapy and a way forward instead of incarceration!

The profile of a female prisoner in Illinois is much the same across America.

1. A woman of color, although the arrest rate of white women is on the rise
2. In her 30s, undereducated, unskilled
4. A victim of sexual abuse, sexual assault, or domestic violence
5. The primary caregiver of dependent children – a single mother
6. Crimes involve drugs and property
7. Has co-occurring psychiatric and substance use disorders

Women commit low-level crimes are not a threat to society. When she does commit a violent crime, it is because she has had enough of the abuse from a spouse, ex-spouse, or boyfriend. Crimes in response to domestic violence and on-going abuse are personal issues, not a risk to community, and should be dealt with as personal issues.

For women, the #1 concern is their children. Stress over worry about their children's well-being, the poor food, the sleeping conditions, not to mention just being locked up, all add to re-traumatization. Most women who have been sexually molested are claustrophobic and confined to a cell without sunshine or exercise adds greatly to her distress.

Considering the type of crimes and their responsibility to their children, most women would be better supervised with community service and a chance at therapy, which is more effective, less costly, and less traumatizing for the family.

Table 12. The rates of suicide and incarceration for the Suicide Belt and the rankings in the world for incarcerating women, and the percentage of children who has an incarcerated parent.

	2019 WOMEN'S INCARCERATION RANKINGS FOR STATES IN THE SUICIDE BELT				
	Suicide[1]	World Incarceration[2]	Women's Incarceration Rates if every state were a country[3]	Female State Imprisonment Rates[4]	Children of Incarcerated Parents[5]
MT	1	21	7	15	8%
AK	2	26	11	11	10%
WY	3	13	2	7	8%
NM	4	15	9	21	10%
ID	5	20	5	4	8%
UT	6	48	31	44	5%
CO	10	32	24	20	5%
NV	11	17	17	13	8%
OK	14	1	1	1	10%
AZ	20	8	12	6	9%

Source: [1]Shaw. (2019). *States with the Highest Suicide Rates.* World Atlas.
[2]Dillinger. (2019). *The most dangerous states in the United States.* World Atlas.
[3]Kajstura & Immarigeon. *States of Women's Incarceration: The global context.* Prison Policy.
[4]*Fact Sheet: Incarcerated women and girls, 1980-2018.* (2018). The Sentencing Project.
[5] Kids Count Data Book (2018). *State Trends in Child Well-Being.*

A three-day stay in jail can ruin a person's chances for future employment and housing. When placed on probation, without the jail time, the consequences are the same. Employers and landlords will not talk to you if you answer yes to the question "have you ever been <u>convicted</u> of a felony or misdemeanor?" (Rodriguez & Emsellem, 2011).

This is important to understand, because even though we talk about three-quarters of the women are on probation as opposed to jail, their lives are affected in the same way. A blemish on your record becomes a cancerous sore before your life is finished.

Young people who go awry with the law are destined for life to low-paying jobs and housing insecurity. Their chances for a professional career are over – most professional organizations, and most major corporations, require a clean record.

> ***When we talk about the people behind America's Iron Curtain of injustice, let us not forget the children and families who are impacted in the same way as if they were incarcerated.***

The struggles encountered by the incarcerated parent entering back into society becomes a minefield for the children who only want a stable home. This instability produces stress in the family, broken families, and severe emotional strain. To reiterate some of these obstacles, consider once again:

- **Barriers to housing.** For someone just released from jail or prison, it is difficult to find safe and stable housing. Policies permit landowners to place blanket bans on renting to ex-inmates, which supports discrimination based on the landowner's ability to "exercise discretion." Housing instability due to frequent moves interrupts the child's secure network of family, friends, and school.

- **Barriers to employment.** The biggest barrier to employment is checking the box on the application that says you committed a crime. That pretty much slams the door for any high-paying job the parent might be qualified for. Lack of training, an interrupted employment history, low literacy, and inadequate education – all are barriers keeping a formerly-incarcerated parent from finding a decent-paying job.

- **Income disparity.** A woman's wages for a job equal to a man's is twenty-two percent less. If a single mom goes to jail, or the father who is the sole support, the family income decreases by one hundred percent.

- **Serious financial problems arise for the parent who is left behind while the other goes to jail.** With the reduction in income, two-thirds of families with a member in prison or jail cannot pay for food, utilities, rent or medical care. Serious debt piles up due to court-related fines and visits to the family member in prison.

- **Lack of help with childcare.** Family members (grandparents) or friends take over the raising of the children while the mom is in jail, for months or years. In many cases, the caregiver either loses her job or quits, because she has no back-up childcare.

- **Inability to care for children.** When a parent is incarcerated, she has no choice but to rely on friends or family to help with her children or put them in foster care. According to the 1997 Adoption and Safe Families Act, if a child is in foster care for fifteen out of the past twenty-two months, the courts can declare the parent unfit. The states continue to lengthen the time of sentencing to longer than fifteen months, and parents spend terms long enough to lose their children. Between 2006 and 2016, 32,000 incarcerated parents had their children permanently taken away without being accused of sexual or physical abuse (Haber & Flagg, 2018).

A parent does not necessarily have to go to jail to be unable to take care of their children. There are other reasons, besides incarceration, that children are placed outside their biological homes. Many go to foster care, some stay with relatives, but the most common blood relative that raises misplaced children are the grandparents.

While incarcerated fathers leave their children with the mother, children with incarcerated mothers usually end up living with a grandmother, a family member, or in foster care.

Grandparents live in neighborhoods where there are few social contacts with children and help with childcare is limited. Even so, children raised by their grandparents have a much easier time than children who are placed in foster homes, where attachment disorders and behaviors make this placement difficult.

In 1999, there were approximately 1.3 million children, or 1.8 percent of the child population, who were cared for by a grandparent without a parent present. In 2017, the U.S. Census reported 5.8 million grandchildren living with 7.3 million grandparents.

> ***In 1995, 1:125 children had a parent in prison or jail, today 1:28 children have a parent behind bars!***
> Annie E. Casey Foundation

Grandparents may have had wealth when they were working, but now they are retired and have a fixed income. The added financial responsibility of raising a child puts a strain on their limited budget, which usually comprises of Social Security and a part-time job.

- Nearly half of families receive cash public assistance, food stamps, or Supplemental Security Insurance (SSI)
- The median annual family income for households without a parent present is $38,964
- Seven of ten grandparents own their own home
- One-third of the grandmothers are not married (Grandchildren)

When your children grow up and leave home, you expect them to take responsibility for their life, make good choices, and be successful in what they do. At first, you know they will be wild and crazy, but that is just the young "feeling their oats." After they get the play out of their system, they want to settle down, get married and have a family. You look forward to having grandkids together for holidays and weekends. You keep the latest pictures of everyone on your phone so you can show them to your friends and brag about how wonderful they are.

This was the way things once worked in American families. There are exceptions, but it seems things do not work out the way we want them to these days. Our grown children leave home and never come back, and we do not know the grandchildren because they live far away. But, when your grown child has a run-in with the law, or drugs play a role in their lives, or your teen comes home pregnant, suddenly there is an unexpected infant in the household and *your* dreams for the future disappear.

Children having children; that is how this world propagates today. It seems people do not understand this concept and think they can have unprotected sex without consequence. Unfortunately, the babies produced from this naivety are cast on the grandparents.

The grandparent's role throughout generations and cultures has been to pass on wisdom and knowledge. Children are meant to be given back to their parents when the visit is over.

Visiting is great, but old age is not for chasing a toddler day in and day out. Raising children is for the young, the ones who can recharge their batteries with a good night's rest.

When a grandparent takes on the raising of their grandchild, they are transported back in time to when their child was a baby. They thought the child raising years were over, and here they are again, back with training pants and training wheels. At my age!

Your dreams of visiting places far and near, or whatever plans you had when your children were raised, are no longer dreams – just dust in the wind. When your friends are out chasing golf balls, you are chasing dust bunnies – just when your kids were small. Except you do not have the energy you used to have. By day's end you are tired…

Why forfeit the dreams you put on hold while your children were growing up and sacrifice comfortable and quiet living for a screaming toddler? Why not tell the parent to take the kid and do what is right? Why not turn your back on what you see and go on with your life? Why have 7.3 million grandparents chosen to raise their children's children?

Answers to those questions would make a book of its own. The next time you see a grandparent struggling with a young child in Walmart, be aware that this child is probably not just visiting grandma for a day or two. The stalwart, patient woman you see is doing this job full time, and her job is not easy.

She inherited a child who is emotionally upset and a behavioral tyrant, she deals with schools that do not understand children who misbehave, her life has turned upside down, and she doubts if she will ever get her sanity back.

The golden years we look forward to are not so golden when you raise someone else's child, even though you love them like your own. Despite the grandparent's own physical- and mental-health issues, despite financial difficulties, living in poverty, stuck in the rut, a child is better off living with a grandparent than with another relative.

Although close kin may provide stable financial security, the emotional support is stronger with a grandparent. Children appreciate their grandparents and seem to fare well in society once they are grown.

In tribute to the millions of kind-hearted souls who have given up their retirement to keep a child off the streets, you are loved and appreciated.

Chapter 9

YOUTH VIOLENCE

When you hear the term "youth violence," what comes to mind?

Neighborhoods ruled by gangs and drive-by shootings? Family fights that turn into domestic violence? Bullies on the playground?

Children are exposed to violence every day.   When you think of youth violence, you picture youth against youth. True, peers can be brutal, but would you believe most of the violence experienced by the young comes from adults? The adults they love and trust.

Forms of violence experienced by children and adolescents:

- Witnessing the arrest of their parent
- Separation from the incarcerated parent
- Child abuse and neglect
- Teen dating violence
- Adult intimate partner violence
- Sexual violence
- Suicide (David-Ferdon et al, 2016)

Children who are mistreated or uprooted from home and family experience severe psychological, emotional, and behavioral problems. If childhood depression, PTSD, panic disorders and eating disorders go unabated, and the symptoms surface as adult chronic diseases such as depression, obesity, cardiovascular and respiratory diseases (Felitti et al, 1998). People with a history of severe abuse as a child can become violent, aggressive, and socially withdrawn; and are at risk for developing an antisocial, borderline, or psychopathic personality disorder.

Imagine the stress for a child who has no roots and a disconnected family. The brain is wired for "normal" events: love, shelter, food, and protection. When these things do not happen, or are disrupted, neurological pathways are disrupted.

The result is feelings of lowered self-worth and helplessness, loss of confidence, and language and development delays – with behaviors surfacing as defiance, a bad attitude, and trouble dealing with school and society (Becker-Weiderman, 2009).

Defiance is defined as deviant and uncontrollable behavior. A traumatized child is a difficult challenge for educators, counselors, parents, and law enforcement. The child is told to make better choices. Misbehavior occurs because the child is coping with extremely high stressors, both internally and externally. When defiance is viewed from a physical standpoint, you see misfiring neurons and neurochemicals running amuck in the brain, and a child making a series of bad choices and difficulty controlling their behavior. (Becker-Weiderman, 2009).

A person's ability to adequately cope with daily life-stressors depends on age and whether the damage happened once or repeatedly. Children who are continually re-traumatized (bullying, abusive home, violent neighborhood, sexual molestation) are at higher risk for developing PTSD (Korn, 2009).

The cues for youth violence begin early in childhood. It is normal for a toddler to exhibit violence through hitting and frustration, but as the child grows, he learns this is not appropriate behavior. He will adapt his responses to receive positive feedback when interacting with others.

There is a subset of children, however, that continue to be aggressive. As they grow older, their impulsivity, poor emotional control, and limited social- and problem-solving skills become a hindrance to their functioning in society. Their behaviors place them at risk for further violence in teen and early adult years – such a picking an abusive mate - and difficulties with socialization and the law (David-Ferdon et al, 2016).

A child's ability to cope with daily life stressors depends on age and whether the damage happened once or repeatedly. Children who are continually retraumatized (bullying, abusive home, violent neighborhood, sexual molestation) are at high risk for developing PTSD (Korn, 2009).

In the Illinois Criminal Justice Information Authority mentioned earlier, the average age of first exposure to physical abuse was 10.3 years, and the average age for first-time sexual abuse was 11.5 years. A family member is first on the list who is likely to sexually abuse a child. About 30% of the perpetrators are known to the victim, an equal number is a stranger. An intimate partner of a parent is next on the list, but only five percent of perpetrators are friends of the victim.

Youth violence and victimization have their roots in community, and the following conditions contributors to childhood maltreatment:

1. Residential instability
2. Crowded housing
3. Density of alcohol-related businesses
4. Poor economic growth or stability
5. Unemployment
6. Concentrated poverty
7. Neighborhood violence and crime
8. Lack of positive relationships among residents
9. Drugs and violence are acceptable behaviors

Children must have academic success and feel connected to their schools; feel positive connections with their parents, teachers, and other caring adults; and interact with prosocial and non-violent peers. This is rather difficult for children whose parents are poor, stressed, live in inadequate housing, and are having trouble with the law.

CHILDREN OF INCARCERATED PARENTS

If we want to end childhood maltreatment and keep kids out of jail, the first thing we need to do is find a different way of dealing with their parents who break the law. We know that most women in prisons and jails are single moms.

Children with a parent behind bars are typically younger than 10 years old, are low-income, and raised by a single mother of color with little educational achievement.

The average age for inmates is between 25 and 44; the age of parents. The number of children with incarcerated parents has risen <u>five hundred percent</u> since 1980! More than five million children have a parent who was incarcerated at some point in their lives (Kids, 2018).

STRESS ON CHILD HEALTH AND WELL-BEING

Incarceration carries the same magnitude of anguish as does abuse, domestic violence and divorce. The Adverse Childhood Experiences Study (ACES), as referred to earlier in the Illinois prison study, is a landmark study that changed the way we understand childhood trauma. Conducted by the Kaiser Permanente Group, it was originally developed to study women who were obese. As the study went on, the researchers discovered commonalities in their subject's childhood backgrounds, such as abuse, domestic violence, parent's divorce, and sexual assault. This discovery led to observing and following 17,000 subjects over the next forty years. What they found resulted in the ACES score card (Felliti et al, 1998).

For the purposes of this paper, the ACES question we will concern ourselves with is:

"Have you had a member of your family incarcerated in jail or prison?"

When a parent goes to jail, the child's support system falls apart. The bond with that parent becomes strained, if not broken entirely. The child harbors doubt, anger, resentment, and worst of all, feelings of abandonment and embarrassment over the parent's legal troubles. The parent is gone from the home for an indeterminate length of time, life spirals downhill, and the child feels lost and alone.

Communication with an incarcerated loved one is expensive. With the high cost of telephone calls and jails limiting the mail to only a postcard, the child does not have much contact with their parent for long periods of time. With separation from the parent comes:

- Depression and anxiety
- Lost interest and achievement in school
- Academic struggles and not graduating from high school
- Lowered teacher expectations because of the child's situation (Kids, 2018)

The child is traumatized because their parent is suddenly taken away, and the police make it worse in the way they arrest the parents. This creates a conundrum for the child. Respect law enforcement out of fear?

> ***One-quarter of children of incarcerated parents are expelled or suspended, as compared to four percent of children of non-incarcerated parents.***
> Glaze & Maruschak. *Parents in Prison and their Minor Children.*
> Bureau of Justice Statistics Special Report

We want our children to obey the law and honor those in authority, and then we expose them to such practices. Of the parents arrested:

- 67 % were handcuffed in front of their children
- 27 % reported weapons drawn in front of their children
- 4.3 % reported a physical struggle in front of their children
- 3.2 % reported the use of pepper spray in front of their children

Children who witness an arrest of a household member are at greater risk of having posttraumatic stress symptoms compared to children who have not witnessed an arrest (Children).

There must be a better way the police can arrest people than exposing children to such practices. Is it any wonder children whose parents spend time in prison or jail grow up with poor mental and physical health – or end up in jail themselves?

STRESS ON THE COMMUNITY AND LOST OPPORTUNITY

Basic economics tell us that for every $1 spent in the community, $3 is generated. Take out one of those dollars and the potential for growth is slashed by one-third. When a breadwinner is incarcerated, not only does the family income drop, but the money available to the community from that worker is also lost.

Poverty and incarceration are causally related. And interestingly, according to Kids Count, living in neighborhoods with a high rate of police calls can cause depression and anxiety for the neighbors!

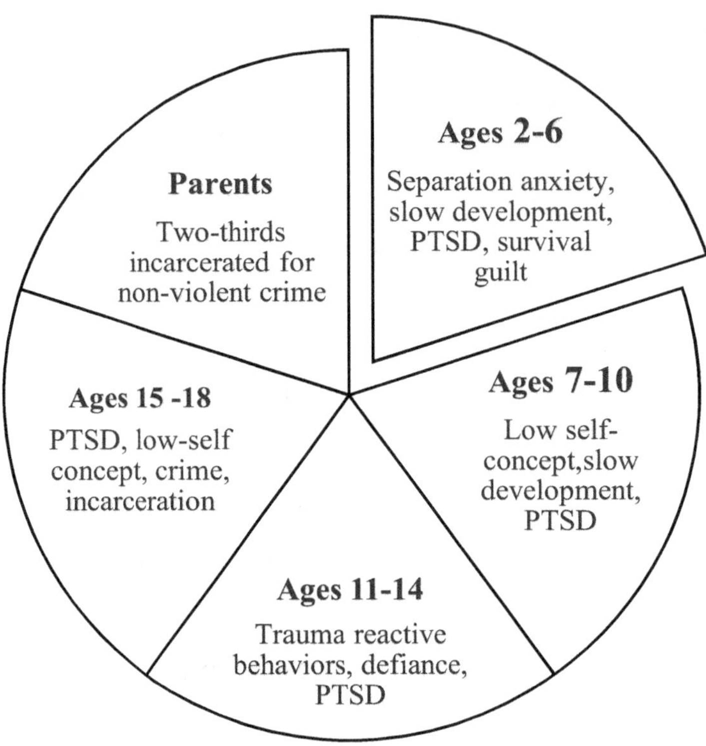

Source: *FAQs about Children of Prisoners*. Prison Fellowship

Countless people caught up in America's justice system say they are not given a fair shake. But when talking to the other side of the law – the attorneys and police – things are going as they should. They are quick to stick up for each other and use scenarios like "maybe they had a good reason" to excuse their actions.

We are naïve about this legal situation in our country – until we are slapped in the face with a tangle with the law. Then our perceptions change.

It is impossible to estimate how many innocent people have been convicted for crimes. People sitting in jail waiting for trial are technically innocent, but are they truly guilty of the crime? There is a world of difference between waiting for the consequences of something you did and waiting for conviction of something you did not do.

A criminal is expected to show remorse for his crime. How does an innocent person feel remorse for a crime they did not commit?

As we move into the next chapters, the tone changes from the conditions of the American family today to how it all began – in the days when Wyoming became a state. To show how the system works, this account shows the tricks used by a deputy, the prosecutor, a judge, and the governor, to send an innocent man to death. These tricks are not new; we have a history of unfair practices against minorities and those we feel should be ostracized. Pull out the history books since the beginning of our country and you will find bigotry and unjust justice.

This way of doing things has led America, the "land of the free," to imprisoning more of her citizens than any other country in the world. And those that suffer the most are the innocent who are proven to be guilty.

Part IV

INCARCERATING AMERICA'S INNOCENT

A devil is still a devil whether he wears a bed sheet or a Brooks Brothers suit.

Malcolm X
Interview with Alex Haley, May 1963

Chapter 10

***I*T *I*S *T*OO *E*ASY TO *C*ONVICT AN *I*NNOCENT *P*ERSON**

It is estimated that wrongful convictions in the U.S. hover around ten percent of the total prison population. Considering there are 2.3 million people in prison, it is staggering to think 230,000 innocent people are in prison.

Best-selling, award-winning author-attorney John Grisham writes riveting fiction novels about the law, courts, judges, and lawyers. His one non-fiction book, *An Innocent Man,* seemed to have changed the course of his life. He is now on the board of directors of the Innocence Project, an organization dedicated to exonerating the wrongfully convicted.

His ah-ha moment came from the story of two white men who were accused of killing two white women in a small town in Oklahoma. The story tells of how the men faced prejudice and roadblocks at every encounter with the judicial system. The police, county attorney and judges ignored the pleas of "I am innocent."

Grisham's book shows how people with mental illness are treated in the correctional system. One man was schizophrenic and was released from the death penalty by the Oklahoma governor at the last hour. If you recall from earlier, Oklahoma is #1 on the list for incarceration rates in the <u>world</u>! After reading Grisham's book, and the way the corrections system handled this case, it is no surprise.

The unfortunate ending to this story, though, is it is not a one-time event in America. This just does not happen to those on death row or convicted for life. They are not the only ones who are proven guilty, even though innocent.

It is easy to gather witnesses and evidence to convict anyone. At this very moment law enforcement could be uncovering the dirt in your life and getting ready to use it against you.

The wrongly convicted are paying not only for a crime they did not commit, but their life takes the same downhill spiral as though they were guilty.

Two-thirds of the jail population are <u>innocent</u> people sitting in jails. Innocent until proven guilty, is that not what we are led to believe? Why are they punished before proven guilty of their crime?

Even if not in jail and out on bond instead, an innocent person faces the recriminations and stigma that goes with criminality in the eyes of the community and family who shun the innocent and doubt their word. "Surely, there must be a reason they are in this trouble," we say to ourselves. Without knowing the facts, we jump to conclusions. It takes a bit of persuasion to convince people of your innocence, especially when the cards are so strongly stacked against you.

Unless there is hard physical evidence (like a body, the stolen money in the thief's pocket, or drugs on their person), it is wrong and inhumane to arrest a person based on assumptions. Law enforcement makes errors in judgement. Witnesses are unreliable. Real crimes are not solved, nor courtrooms run, in such an easy manner as the Hollywood crime shows. But the law does work when people do their jobs. Corruption and cutting corners are neither necessary nor ethical.

The pitfall with law enforcement and prosecuting attorneys pushing for guilty convictions is that they can get it wrong. Supposedly the legal system is set up to protect the innocent, but the people who are convicted of crimes they did not commit will not agree with you.

When a family member is raped or murdered, the family craves justice. These horrible crimes touch not only the victim, but also the people closest to them. The perpetrator is arrested and found guilty in a court of law. What more can anyone ask?

The system works well if the convicted is truly guilty of the crime. Another bad guy off the streets. But what happens if the convicted is innocent? The murderer or rapist is still free, feeling cocky because he got away with another one.

The family of the victim thinks they found justice because the killer is behind bars, but this is a false sense of security. The perpetrator, however, is still raping and killing other members of society.

When a prosecutor or law enforcement officer pushes strongly for a conviction, their ego is more involved than their concern for what is right and wrong. They are geared toward winning their case, and less passionate about convicting the right person. Public defenders are overworked and will see their client one or two times before a hearing - inadequate information and not enough time to hear their client's story.

One innocent person convicted of a crime is one too many

Unfortunately, convicting innocent people is nothing new. The story you are about to read is recorded in the annals of Wyoming history and is a fitting example of how the law can ruin someone's life. It contains childhood maltreatment, suicide, incarceration, and the wrongly convicted; lynchings, vigilantes, and politics over justice; yellow journalism; and a woman scorned and impugned for her attempts to right a serious wrong. Above all, this true story shows how Wyoming's justice system operated much the same 120 years ago as it does today.

What significance does a crime committed over a century ago have to do with the topic of this book? The significance is not in the crime, but the way the politicians, attorneys, and the deputy handled the situation. History buffs will enjoy this brief journey into the past, but the point is to set the scene. Tom Horn waited 120 years to have his true story told.

. "They will tell (the truth) sometime, but I can't benefit much from it if they tell it after I am hanged."

To begin, a brief history of the years before Wyoming became a state with women's suffrage and the Homestead Act setting the stage for settlement. Between 1870 and 1900, Wyoming boasted having the largest cattle industry in the world. Free land, no fences, the cattlemen claimed the prairie and the homesteaders were invaders. Most were honest folk just starting a new life, but the bad apples were rustlers who stole stock from the cattlemen. This led to lynchings and vigilantes, the stuff that made legends of the Wild West. The relevance of each piece of history will come to light as the story evolves.

Here is the truth behind the saga of Tom Horn.

If you have made it this far through this book, and still believe the criminal justice system is fair, then perhaps his story will change your mind.

FREE LAND!

In 1862, President Lincoln signed the Homestead act which gave 160 acres to each registered voter – if they could meet the conditions. First the claim had to be staked out and filed, then the homesteader had five years to make improvements such as building a house, putting in crops, and running livestock. If the homesteader survived the five years, the land was his, free and clear.

The people who took advantage of this "free land" Act were adventurous types looking for a challenge - Civil War veterans; soldiers from the western fronts; farmers wanting better land (Surprise! The land in Wyoming is arid and rocky); and the many cowboys and drovers laid off from their jobs as the cattle industry began to wane. By 1900, a quarter of all homesteaders were foreign born (Sodaro & Adams, 1998). Many natives of Wyoming are first- and second-generation Americans with parents and grandparents who immigrated during this time to Wyoming from Europe and Russia to escape the upcoming war.

There were plenty of challenges to living in this wild western territory. Prairie fires would wipe out a crop and a homestead in a flash; swarms of grasshoppers destroyed crops in minutes. Hot dry winds in the summer, freezing winds and blizzards in the winter. Winter travel was nearly impossible, and people would hunker in their cabins for months at a time. The few doctors were miles away when you most needed them; women died in childbirth and many infants did not live past their first year. But despite all these possible avenues to failure, if people could survive the elements, they managed to eke out a living and build their homesteads.

Women having the right to vote and owning land was very advantageous for homesteaders – a couple could claim 320 acres – 160 acres for the wife and 160 acres for the husband, and more if the children were over 21. This is how many ranches and large farms in the Wyoming were started, but it was not an easy task. Most people did not make their five-year requirement, simply because the conditions were too harsh.

THE CATTLE BARONS RULE

In 1867, the Union Pacific Railroad completed its line to Cheyenne, Wyoming. This was a boon for the cattle rancher. When cattle were driven (herded) to Oregon to sell, they lost weight on the way. Now the cattlemen could load up their fattened cattle on trains (without fear of them losing weight) and ship them to Chicago where they would sell for $7 a head (Sodaro & Adams, 1998).

From the 1870's to 1900, Wyoming sported the largest cattle operation in the world. Cattle barons ruled the land. All that free government land, no fences, and cows being relatively maintenance free – it was a dream for the money mongers. The prices for beef were high and the overhead was ridiculously low, thanks to the open range and free forage.

In 1873, the Swan Land and Cattle Company was incorporated at Chugwater, Wyoming, and began with 3,000 head of cattle. At its peak, Swan was the largest livestock operation in the history of the west. By 1886, the Swan Company owned 1.5 million cattle worth $54 million. The Company held land ninety miles east of Cheyenne to Sidney, Nebraska, and ninety miles northwest of Cheyenne to Rock River, Wyoming. There were so many brands, they had their own published book.

The years between 1876 and 1886 are called the "Great Grass Bonanza." The high profits attracted investors from all over the world. During this time, there were over two hundred cattle companies in Wyoming (Sodaro & Adams, 1996).

Heavily overstocked and overgrazed, the vegetation on the land was giving out. The final blow, though, was the winter of 1886-87. With temperatures of minus 50 degrees and three to four feet of snow on the ground, the cattle herds were wiped out and many a fortune was ruined.

THE WARREN MACHINE

Judge Joseph M. Carey came to Wyoming in 1867 as the presidential-appointed District Attorney. He served from 1871 to 1876 on the Wyoming Supreme Court and was referred to as "Judge" Carey thereafter. He served as the national Republican chairman from 1876 to 1897. Carey was a United States Senator when Wyoming became a state but was so consumed by his cattle business that he was little help in other areas of politics. He was instrumental in planning and financing the Johnson County War, and lost favor with his Republican supporters because of it. But he was a popular public figure, and served as Democratic governor from 1911 to 1915. His political career dimmed because of a rivalry with Senator Francis E. Warren, who controlled the state Republican party.

Francis E. Warren was a Civil War veteran and was awarded the Medal of Honor at age 19. He moved to Wyoming in 1868 and quickly saw possibilities for both financial and political success. Cattleman and businessman, he served as territorial governor for two terms and was the first elected governor to Wyoming in 1890. He served this term for six weeks, then was elected United States Senator, which he held for the next thirty-eight years.

He was known for his "pork barrel policies," - appropriating federal money for local projects. He built a political structure that was unbeatable, better known as the "Warren Machine." Along with many other politicians, including Warren's one-time political friend turned serious rival, Judge Carey, Warren was involved in the cattle industry. The flavor ran high for the cattlemen in the political world.

CATTLE WERE BIG BUSINESS, AND BUSINESS WAS BOOMING

Cattlemen and homesteaders did not mingle well. The big cattle outfits felt the settlers were taking precious land and water resources, invading the free grazing areas, and were generally a nuisance to the cattle barons. The settlers were claiming the bottom lands that had the water. Water is scarce in Wyoming. The best places to start a homestead was on the bottomland – the land around the rivers.

Many of the settlers were old cowboys who lost their jobs to the big outfits that had their own crew and needed fewer hands. Some of these retired cowboys saw the best way to build their herds was to "borrow" cattle from the large outfits. They would cover the original brand with their own, and sell them at market.

The cattlemen were furious because they were losing cattle, and the public land they claimed as their own was being invaded. Something had to be done, not only to stop the rustlers, but also to drive out the settlers. Lynchings and shootings were uncomfortably common, and the courts always ruled in favor of the rustlers.

The settlers were furious because they were harassed by the cattlemen. The big herds passing by would pick up the settlers' small herd, and their stock (income and food) would be gone. The cattlemen poisoned streams and fenced off the water in their intent to drive the homesteaders off the land.

The Wyoming Stock Growers Association (WSGA) was formed in 1879 by the ranchers to protect their interests. By 1885, the association had grown to 360 members with two million head of cattle (Gould, 1989). The cattlemen controlled who could sell cattle when and where, and blackballed the settlers to prevent them from buying and selling their cattle (Sodaro & Adams, 1996). The courts and judges were lenient with the cattle thieves, and the juries were made up of rustlers. In frustration, the cattlemen "looked to themselves," and decided to take whatever measures were necessary to solve the problem.

In 1884, The "Maverick Law" appointed the WSGA as the official agent for the government-run roundups of the maverick cattle. Unbranded, unclaimed cattle running loose on the range were called "mavericks." At the roundups, these cattle were branded and sold at auction. The money from these sales financed the bulk of the WSGA operations, including hiring stock detectives and brand inspectors. All the officials were cattlemen, and it looked like this law was meant to protect the big ranchers.

President Cleveland put a kibosh on some of the activity with his Land Reform bill of 1885. He saw the railroads and cattlemen getting out of hand and felt public domain should be protected from "purloining schemes and unlawful occupation" (Gould, 1989).

1. Cattlemen were checked in their abuses
2. Railroad grants were supervised with greater care
3. Timber depredations were halted and past offenses prosecuted
4. Surveying and private land claims protected
5. Large areas were selected for public use

You can imagine the furor this caused among the cattle and railroad barons! Grazing land reduced, fences in place! Regulations to follow!

VIGILANTES AND HOMESTEADERS

In 1891, a Board of Livestock Commissioners was formed, and secretly began to explore ways to eliminate rustlers and settlers from open range (Sodaro & Adams, 1998). People will fight over anything, and in this case, it was about overgrazed land and scarce water. Several prominent cattlemen, including Frank Canton and Senator Carey, financed and planned a raid on Johnson County. Carey encouraged the plan, but when trouble started, he deserted them.

The Commission hired twenty Texas lawmen to come to Wyoming to eliminate the rustlers. Once in Cheyenne, the Texans met up with twenty-four cattlemen from Wyoming, and on April 5, 1892, a posse of forty-four men set out for Johnson County (Gould, 1989).

They had a list of people to kill. The vigilantes murdered the first two men, and the chase was on. The plan backfired. Not to be cowed, the Sheriff of Johnson County, William "Red" Angus, gathered settlers to defend against the forty-four (the reported number of settlers that joined Red varies from 200 to 400, depending on the source).

The settlers cornered the vigilantes at the TA Ranch on Crazy Women Creek and held them for two days. Just when they were getting ready to launch an attack, Territorial Governor Amos Barber saved the day. He appealed to President Harrison to send an army regiment to arrest the forty-four men. Johnson County did not have the funds to finance such a large trial, or to house that many men. The men were escorted to Fort D.A. Russell (Warren Airforce Base) in Cheyenne, where they were held for several months. Eventually, the Texans went back to Texas and the Wyoming vigilantes dispersed into the wind. No one was convicted.

In July 1899, the night before the Wyoming Constitutional Convention signed the document for Statehood that would be sent to Congress for approval, Jim Averel and Cattle Kate were lynched for rustling cattle. This, and lynchings and shootings of several other rustlers, set the scene for Wyoming's launch into statehood.

Needless to say, the new State of Wyoming had a violent beginning. The rustlers were stealing cattle and the cattlemen were lynching rustlers. People slept with guns and carried them while they went about their day.

In May 1882, after the Johnson County War, while working for the Pinkerton Detective agency, Tom Horn investigated the ambush and murder of deputy U.S. Marshall George Wellman, that occurred around the time of the Johnson County War. He then went to work for John Coble, a foreman of the Swan Land and Cattle Company and Two-Bar Ranch.

> ***"I then came to Wyoming and went to work for Swan Land and Cattle Company,
> since which time everybody else has been more familiar with my life and business
> than I have been myself."***
> Tom Horn (Himself, 1904)

In another attempt to protect their interests, cattleman Frank Canton requested the Pinkerton Detective Agency to send a man to help end the rustling. The Pinkerton's was the largest detective agency in the world, contracting out to hunt outlaws and provided private security for large firms such as the railroads. Even though he was no longer in their employ in April of 1895, the Denver office referred Horn to Canton as the man who could work with the cattlemen.

Legend has Horn murdering seventeen men during his lifetime. The experts on the subject say Tom was a braggart and loved to tell tall tales. They say his autobiography is a fantasy, and he was not as mild-mannered as he pictured himself to be. I am not an expert on Tom Horn's life, my knowledge comes from what has been recorded by others. I have done my best to be objective and open-minded, to weigh out the negative and damaging reviews, and to give him a chance as a man. Did he kill seventeen men? Did he push the Army officers around? Was his story written to pass the time while waiting for the noose, and not an actual autobiography? Was Tom Horn full of it?

His story is a shining example of how someone innocent of a crime can be blackballed and backed into a corner. It is difficult to sort the truth from the lies in the story of Tom Horn, but one thing is certain, he was hung for a crime he did not commit.

Someone shot 14-year-old Willie Nickell on July 17, 1901. The State of Wyoming tried and convicted him, and hanged him until dead on November 20, 1903, one day before his forty-third birthday.

Through the twists and turns resulting from an overzealous deputy U.S. Marshall, a politically-driven county attorney, a governor more worried about public opinion and his political rise than doing the right thing, and a jury that was threatened by the public if they did not convict Horn, a great lie was built to make him look guilty. Add to this, Warren's political machine, cattlemen never having their due in court, and yellow journalism keeping the sparks alive, Tom Horn never had a chance. He suspected he had been jobbed as soon as he was arrested.

"I knew in my own mind that I would lose from the first time I went to trial."

"The governor's decision was no surprise to me, for I was tried, convicted, and hung before I left the ranch. My famous confession was also made days before I came to town."
Tom Horn in a letter to his friend, John Coble, while awaiting execution.

He wrote a colorful autobiography of his life while in jail, but stopped his narrative at his arrival in Wyoming. If his story is a lie, how could he describe the things he did if he did not see for himself the massive Indian tribes that were running from American soldiers, and be able to describe in great detail their customs and how they dressed? One thing is sure, he was a master craftsman at making lariats, ropes, and hackamores from horsehair. He learned this craft while living with the Apaches, and it was a valued pastime for him during the twenty-two months he was in the Laramie County Jail.

Little men cannot encompass the broadness of the experiences of such men, and so they make their accomplishments seem small. For nearly twenty years, Tom lived in both a military and Indian culture, where a man's word was trusted, and honor was a daily practice. When he came to Wyoming, he was not prepared for the graft and corruption that caused his doom

Chapter 11

CRUSHED BETWEEN THE GRINDSTONES OF TWO CIVILIZATIONS

Born November 21, 1860 near Memphis, Missouri, Horn spent his early years hunting game in the woods with his dog, Shed. He loved to track and hunt a great deal more than going to school. Even at a young age he was an expert shot, and his mother would send him to hunt dinner for his family and the neighbors. Despite his yearning for the outdoors, he became educated, and his mother made sure he had a religious upbringing. He also received regular thumpings from his father just to keep him in line.

Two events within a short time set him on his course for life. Upon getting in an argument with two boys about his dog, one of them shot and killed Shed. Tom was devastated at the loss of his only friend and constant companion. Shortly after this, Tom informed his father he was leaving home. His father told him he could leave after he recovered from the beating he was going to give him. It took Tom a week to recover, he kissed his mother goodbye, and headed out West on foot with only a lunch and a few dollars in his pocket. He was 13 years old.

It took him a year to get to Santé Fe, New Mexico. While travelling, he learned to speak Spanish, and he said he grew up more in that year than any other time (Himself, 1904). After taking odd jobs riding shotgun for different outfits, he met up with Al Sieber when he was around 15 years old. Sieber was the head scout for the U.S. Army for the southwestern area, and seeing a promise in the boy, he took Tom under his wing and taught him the finer tricks of scouting. Tom also lived for a time with an Apache tribe, where he learned to speak the language and was accepted as one of them. His mastery of the two languages made him invaluable as an interpreter. Although Sieber had no trouble with the languages, Tom became his right-hand man.

Tom earned an excellent reputation as a scout and interpreter, and worked for the Army in this capacity on and off, as appropriations allowed, for the next fifteen years of the Indian wars. Later, he worked a silver mine, sold his claim, and first came to Wyoming in 1892.

In 1896, he went back to Arizona and was involved in a cattle/rustler war there. He contacted yellow fever in Cuba during the Spanish American War and came back to recover at the Two Bar ranch in Wyoming in 1899 or early 1900.

Lawman, army interpreter, scout during the Indian wars, champion bronc buster, Pinkerton man, deputy U.S. Marshall, stock detective, mule packer for the Spanish American war. In the preface to his autobiography, John Coble wrote:

> Note his unerring memory, even to minute details; the objects of his hero worship and the sort of men they were; his unconsciously expressed forgiveness for injuries; an untiring faithfulness to duty under the most trying circumstances; his strong sense of justice; and note particularly that although his manuscript was written to hurry lagging time, and for the private perusal of his friends only, it contains not the slightest strain of vulgarity. No expurgation has been necessary.
>
> Himself, 1904

Aide-de-camp Marion Maus served in Arizona during the Indian wars where he received a Medal of Honor for his service, had a long history of valor, and ended his career as Brigadier General. Horn was with Maus as an Indian scout when pursuing Geronimo, and in Cuba during the Spanish-American War. Maus wrote in his letter to the Quartermaster General from Army Headquarters on February 28, 1899, that Tom Horn was one of the bravest men he knew. Horn was with Maus in the Indian Wars in Arizona and was a commander of the scouts during the Mexican/Apache conflict in the Sierra Madre Mountains. He spoke Spanish fluently, and was invaluable as a scout, or packer, cow herder, packer. Maus stated Horn was an all-around good man and had high regard for him as chief of scouts (Carlson, 2001).

In an incident in Reno, Nevada, in 1891, where he was tried for stealing money, and found not guilty, his defense attorney secured several dispositions attesting to his character, including ones from General Nelson A Miles, ex-sheriffs, U.S. Marshalls and judges. All vouched that Tom was an honest and steadfast, and had never suspected dishonesty (Gould, 1989).

His friend and employer, John Coble, believed in Tom's innocence enough that he financed his trial, and at the end, arranged for the funeral and bought the casket.

How could a man with Horn's experience, characteristics, and high acclaim from the people he worked with before he came to Wyoming, how could a man suddenly turn so bad he goes on a killing spree? Never once during his trial was mention made of his past.

Horn was a master tracker during the time when the government prevailed and set aside reservations for the Indians to live on. The Natives did not accept this very well. The government chose some of the worst land, rousted them from their homelands, and sent them to places foreign to their lifestyle.

These tribes had lived on this continent for thousands of years and had their customs and way of life suited a certain area. When they were placed on reservations, all of that was taken away from them and they had to start their lives over again. The Natives were skilled warriors, they outweighed the soldiers both in fighting skill and numbers of men. Moving them onto reservations was not an easy task for the Army.

The Indian scouts contracted out to the Army to follow the tribes and report their whereabouts. Al Sieber, Tom's friend and mentor was respected among the Indians and their chiefs. He spent most of his time convincing the leaders to give in peacefully.

The Indians hated reservation life. They were starving because their rations were stolen by the agents and sold to the settlers. The promises of the government to help them proved to be false, and many of the tribes escaped the reservations and went to Mexico. The scout's job was to find them and report their whereabouts to the Army.

When Horn took on the job as stock detective, he used the same tactics he used as a scout. He was expert at watching and waiting. As his verdict was read said he showed little emotion. The newspapers described him to be stoic, like an Indian. He was a man caught between two worlds – just and unjust.

His system that never failed did not include killing men. Only conjecture ties Horn to any of the men that were murdered. Such stories of Horn's prowess ran rampant for a reason. Newspapers reported that Horn killed men and left them to lie, rumors spread by ranchers said the same.

Horn carefully fostered his reputation.
"That is my stock in trade."
Glendolene Kimmel (Himself, 1904)

The only inquest into any of the suspected killings, beside the Nickell murder, was of two men, Rash and Dart, which did not find evidence pointing to Horn.

By his admission, Horn intentionally made a reputation for himself that would induce fear. He knew the power of fear and used it. He bragged about his prowess as a paid assassin to carry his image. In an age when most men were less than six feet tall, he towered over them at six feet, one inch. His size alone was intimidating.

No one knows for sure if he ever killed anyone, but he did not kill Willie Nickell.

"As far as actual killing is concerned, I never killed a man in my life,
or a boy, either."
Tom Horn at his trial, under oath

He used scare tactics. "Drop that knife or I'll put a bullet in your head." One couple reported opening their shade at night after hearing a scratch on their window and there stood Tom Horn. That sounds odd, but the long dark Wyoming nights have been known to conjure up some strange and scary imaginings.

> "I got there when the stealing was going on. I associated myself so directly with the neighborhood that stealing cannot go on with me being present. If they steal, I will catch them in the act…When I would find a man stealing my (employers) calf, of people I represented, I would simply take the calf…Such things as that stopped stealing."

What was life like working as a stock detective? Riding the range was a seasonal job. The weather was warm, and for someone accustomed to traveling light, the meager belongings Tom carried while on the trail was not unusual.

It was customary for cowboys on the range to use an army blanket for a saddle blanket, and sleep under the stars with the blanket as a cover and their saddle for a pillow. Tom kept stashes of bacon tied up in trees or would shoot a jackrabbit for dinner. When he arrived at the Millers, he had only the clothes he was wearing, his .30-30 Winchester, and a pair of binoculars.

126

Iron Mountain, aptly named, contains vast stores of iron, and carries an ominous history. Fifty square miles bordered on all sides by large cattle ranches. It was originally surveyed in 1876 by Frank Canton, who was a surveyor for the federal government. (A rather shifty man who was instrumental in the invasion of Johnson County, and who requested the stock detective from the Pinkerton Agency.) He was convicted of selling false claims while surveying Iron Mountain. The Union Pacific later built a railroad to bring out the ore, a road was built, and these two amenities attracted homesteaders to the area.

Two of these settlers and their families were Jim Miller and Kels Nickell. The Millers had seven children: Among the oldest children in 1901 was Gus age 19, and Victor 18. A younger boy, 13-year-old Frank, was accidentally shot in the head in August 1900, from a loaded weapon, and his 9-year-old sister, Maude's face was severely damaged, but she survived.

The Nickell's had eight children: The oldest, Julie 18, was married; Frank, age 17 was away in Kentucky at a boarding school; and Willie was 14. The Millers settled in the area in 1873; the Nickells in 1875. Both men were hard workers and built sizable spreads, complete with large herds of cattle (Horn later testified they started their herds by rustling from Coble's herd). These two men fought about everything. There were threats between the two, and they would tell whoever would listen one was going to kill the other.

Kels Nickell sold his cattle, and in May of 1901 he put in 3,000 head of sheep. The cattlemen hated sheep. They thought sheep ate down the grass so short that the cattle could not get to it. This has long been a misconception and has caused many a trouble between cattlemen and woolgrowers.

The truth is, sheep have different nutritional needs than cows, but the cattlemen did not know this then. The problem was overgrazing. Too many livestock on dry, arid prairie land and not enough grass to feed them all.

Kels created an uproar when he brought sheep to Iron Mountain. People said he would not live until 1902 if he brought those sheep in. Kels, being the kind of man he was, did not care what his neighbors thought, and it was consensus among his neighbors that he brought in the sheep out of spite.

One thing led to another, and in June of 1901, Jim Miller whipped Willie Nickell with a switch, threatened to shoot his horse, and then told son Victor to "lick" him.

Tom Horn came into the area the Monday evening before Willie's murder, checking on Coble's pastures and looking for rustlers. He spent the night at Millers, and Tuesday morning had breakfast with the family and the schoolteacher who was living there, Glendolene Kimmel. Later that morning, he and the Millers went fishing and practiced shooting at targets. Jim Miller noted that Tom was "the worst shot he'd ever seen" (Davis, 2016). Whether that was a boastful statement, or if Horn was stroking Miller's ego will never be known, but both men were excellent shots. They discovered that day that Horn and Victor Miller both had .30-30 Winchesters, used the exact same bullets, and bought them from the same place (Bowers, 2004).

Tuesday afternoon, Horn reported that the Nickell's sheep were next to Miller's potato patch. Tom left Wednesday morning, went up across the divide of the Sybille and Chugwater Rivers, checked the pastures for signs of rustling, and rode back to the Two Bar on Saturday. After eating a good meal, taking care of business, and cleaning up from a week on the range, he went into Laramie, Wyoming, where he proceeded on to a ten-day drunk.

Early Thursday morning, July 18, 1901, 14-year-old Willie was sent out by Kels to look for a stranger that had passed through looking for work. Willie did not come home that night, which was not of concern as it was common for him to stay at a neighboring ranch. The next morning, his younger brother found him about three-quarters of a mile from the house, dead from three bullet wounds.

"Had he been on a murderous errand, he would not have shown himself."
Glendolene Kimmel (Himself, 1904)

NO GOOD DEED GOES UNPUNISHED

There were plenty of people who did not feel Horn killed Willie. It was a general belief throughout the Iron Mountain community that the bullets that killed Willie were meant for Kels.

Despite the aspersions cast in the courtroom and in the press, people liked Tom. He was likable, smart, polite. Several people come forth with affidavits declaring his innocence after he was convicted, but the one that stood up the loudest for him was the schoolteacher, Glendolene Kimmel.

Back in the day of the one-room schoolhouse, teachers were recruited to come to Wyoming. Several families built the schoolhouse, and the schoolteacher lived among them. This was the case with the Iron Mountain school that was built by both by the Millers and the Nickells, and the children from both families attended (the one thing they did together without fighting). Ten children were enrolled in the school, but children helped at home during busy times, like branding and calving, and planting and harvesting. Attendance at the school was low during these times.

Glendolene was in her early 20s when she came to Wyoming as a "schoolmarm." She came from a prominent family in Missouri, was well educated and socially refined. She was told about the Miller/Nickell feud before she accepted the job, was advised not to take it, but she was interested in studying human behavior and wanted to learn about the frontier type. She did not know what she was getting in to.

There was a group of young women at the turn of the twentieth century who were not suffragettes, but they enjoyed the freedom and the newness of having a career instead of marriage. Wyoming women could vote and hold property, and this was an appealing draw for many. Glendolene thought she was coming to a progressive state where she could enjoy the amenities of freedom that were not allowed in elsewhere in America.

She arrived in Cheyenne in January of 1901, but did not move to Iron Mountain until July when she started teaching school.

In Glendolene's 1903 affidavit, she states that she was suspicious something was wrong the day Willie died. Kels approached her at the schoolhouse and told her Willie had been killed, and blamed the Millers. She said she did not know anything about it and wanted to talk to the Millers first. When she had Gus, Victor and Mrs. Miller together, she told them about Willie, and Mrs. Miller talked about their troubles with the Nickells.

Victor snapped at his mom, telling her to be quiet because Glendolene would tell the court everything they said against the Nickells. Glendolene thought this was rather odd. Victor was an uncomplicated country boy, and later stated his comments and evasiveness aroused her suspicions. That evening, the Millers had an impromptu dance and get-together with some of the neighbors. An effort to appear normal?

When a prosecuting attorney has no clue who committed the crime, they start looking to any suitable suspect. Before DNA and forensic medicine, solving a murder was even more of a guessing game than it is today. To try to determine the facts, the courts held a coroner's inquest. This panel was comprised of three citizens appointed by the county attorney and the coroner. It was an informal affair, anyone on the panel could ask questions, and only people that managed to show up were questioned, but not sworn in (Davis, 2016).

Glendolene had been at the Miller's three weeks when the coroner's inquest began. She was not a trusted member of the family; the Millers were guarded around her and had not spoken ill of the Nickell family in her presence. She testified the Miller family were all present at breakfast the day Willie was killed, but later stated they ate anywhere between 7 and 9 a.m., and she remembered Victor being late.

On Saturday, August 3, sheep once again trespassed onto the Miller's land, driven there by Kels' sheepherder. The sheepherder testified at the second inquest that Miller threatened to "fix the son of a bitch before daylight."

On Sunday, August 4, 1901, someone fired five shots at Kels when was milking his cows; three struck him but did not kill him. His two younger daughters said they saw two men on horseback, one bigger than the other, ride away on what looked like the Miller's horses. When his daughter, Julia, and neighbor Joe Reed, returned from taking Kels to the hospital in Cheyenne, they found fifty to sixty sheep clubbed, crippled, and gutted. Nothing was ever proven. Victor, Gus, and Jim Miller were arrested, but were later released. It is unclear why – supposedly they had an alibi.

At the second inquest on August 9, Glendolene stated that if someone were pushing sheep on to her land, she would have shot them.

But she was hearing things that disturbed her. When Stoll questioned her on her thoughts of the situation, she said she learned both Jim and Kels were bad men. When Stoll asked her to expound on her observations, she tagged the two quite accurately. One was slower and obstinate, the other quick and fiery. She felt a man of different character would have ignored Nickell, or a different man would have ignored Miller. Of course, they had trouble as they were the same type of men. Horn confirmed this in his testimony, saying the two men would complain to the neighbors about their troubles and how ornery the other was (Carlson, 2001).

A CONSPIRACY

Prosecuting attorney Walter Stoll was unsuccessful in ferreting out Willie's murderer in the coroner's inquest, and it was time to turn up the heat. Laramie County Commissioner Chairman, Sam Corson, secretly struck a deal with lawman Joe Lefors to find Willie's killer, and offered him $1000, with payment of the award money split between the county and state.

In his autobiography, Lefors related that he told Corson the reason Willie was killed was because of the range war, and if he could find the outfit with the largest financial investment in the area, he would find the killer.

The outfit with the most cattle in the Iron Mountain area was, of course, John Coble and the Two-Bar Ranch, a branch of the Swan Cattle Company. The outfit that employed Tom Horn; the man with questionable killings in his background, and who, as we shall see, was a much better man than Lefors.

According to Lefors, there was another reason John Coble would be a perfect suspect for hiring an assassin for Kels. This feud between the landowners on Iron Mountain, mostly fueled by Miller and Nickells, went way back. Kels always had an explosive temper, and in July of 1890, he got into an altercation with Coble and his foreman, and stabbed Coble in the abdomen with a knife. Lefors easily used this incident to further cement his suspicions. Add to that Horn's suspected history of killing other men, Lefors knew exactly where he would start.

At the Cheyenne Frontier Days in August 1901, while Horn was placing first in the riding and roping competitions, Lefors was busy working the case. Lefors told Horn he would split the $1000 reward money with him if they could convict the person who murdered Willie.

In her affidavit, Glendolene reported Jim Miller said he saw Lefors during the Cheyenne Frontier Days who said to him,

> "…when Tom Horn was brought to trial, if he (Miller) would take the stand against Tom Horn; that Joe Lefors would personally see to it that neither Miller nor any member of the family would be held responsible for the murder of Nickell, and that further, Lefors would give Miller five hundred dollars – out of the reward money. Miller further said to me that he saw through Lefors' game; that Lefors didn't care anything for him; that if he did what Lefors wanted him to and Tom Horn was convicted, he would never get any of the money, and he might be hanged 'alongside of Tom Horn'."

In his autobiography, Lefors said Jim offered him $500 dollars to keep quiet about Willie. Both men were dishonorable, so which story do you believe? Jim Miller was confident that Victor would not be implicated, which appears certain this conversation between Lefors and Miller occurred, but who offered who money will never be known.

It was also said Jim Miller offered a $500 diamond for the killing of Kels and there was also off-handed talk that Miller asked Horn to "take care" of Kels.

THE REAL KILLER IS REVEALED

In the first part of September, Glendolene heard Jim and Victor talking about the murder, saying that since no one had accused them, they must be in the clear. The Miller house was arranged so that her bedroom was next to the parlor where the family spent most of their time. As was customary at the time (no computers, TVs, or cell phones), the family would sit around the table at night, reading the mail, playing cards, and discussing the day's events. Since her bedroom was right off the parlor, she clearly heard the conversations between Jim and Victor after the rest of the family went to bed. They must have forgotten they could be heard through the thin walls and open doorways.

On three occasions during September, Glendolene heard conversations between Victor and Jim about the murder. She approached Jim Miller near the end of September and told him what she had heard. She told him Victor was a product of the circumstances, the people responsible for the trouble were Jim and Kels, and considering Victor's young age of 18, she felt it best to watch and wait.

By October she had had enough of the Wyoming life. On October 10, 1901, she resigned her position at the school and left Iron Mountain for good. She had been employed as a teacher for 105 days. She must have been terrified, living in a house with such angry people and knowing one of them killed a young boy and would not come forth. After telling Jim what she knew, followed by her sudden departure, did she fear her life was in danger, as well?

When Victor was taking her to Cheyenne to put her on the train to go back to Missouri, she told him what she knew and again said she felt he was a victim of the circumstances. Both Jim and Victor told her the same thing; Willie and Victor came upon one another that morning, they got into a squabble, Victor had his ever-present gun, and shot Willie.

Willie was not shot from up close, as if in a scuffle, but from a distance away, as if someone were lying in wait. The ballistics experts at the trial testified that the bullets made a downward path through the boy's body. The shooter was hidden in an outcropping sixty yards from the gate where Willie dismounted his horse to close the gate. He had his back to the outcropping when he was shot. He walked sixty-five feet toward his home until he fell in the dirt face first. The shooter then walked up and turned his body over, as evidenced by the gravel, blood, and dirt on the front of Willie's body, and left a size 7 or 8 boot print at the scene.

Before Glendolene left Cheyenne on October 11, 1901, she tried twice that day to contact Stoll to tell him what she knew, but both times he was in court. She left Wyoming alone with this knowledge. This was not the end of her involvement with proclaiming Tom's innocence. But it was obvious she was safer watching from a vantage point far away from the lynchings and rustlers. What a welcome to Wyoming she had!

Shortly after her return to Missouri, on November 10, 1901, she filed the following affidavit:

"I, Glendolene Myrtle Kimmell, being first duly sworn upon my oath, depose and say that I now have positive knowledge as to who killed William Nickell, and he was not killed by Tom Horn. If a new trial is granted in this case of the State of Wyoming versus Tom Horn, I will attend such trial and testify with facts, as above stated."

The coroner's inquest went from July into September, 1901, with Walter Stoll presiding. Kels was adamant one of the Millers killed his son. At first Stoll thought so, too. As the questioning went on, no one came forth and confessed, but the feud between the two men commanded the session.

Stoll questioned Horn extensively to his whereabouts. Horn's answers were consistent throughout, and from a position of a lawman who was helping solve the murder.

Not able to spot the liar out of the bunch, Stoll began making assumptions. And from then on, the case was based on assumptions and circumstances, with no hard evidence pointing to Horn.

By the nature of Horn's job, he had only his word of where he was Thursday morning. Add in a confession taken under the most unlawful manner, coerced through trickery after a two-day all-night drinking binge, the letter of the law turned sour for Tom.

Always a man with a strong sense of justice, never a man who trusted the system, he stated during his trial he would trust cattle over courts anytime.

JOBBED!

Tom never drank before coming to Wyoming, as reported by his colleagues and commanding officers. He accompanied Al Seiber on his campaigns to stop the Indians from making mescal, a potent alcoholic drink from the agave plant. When he found an Indian with a still, Al destroyed the still and chased the offender away. Tom saw firsthand the dangers alcohol brought to the tribes. His previous employers said Tom never drank, but when he came back to Wyoming after recovering from yellow fever, there are several accounts of him getting into trouble while drinking. What caused this change in Tom's behavior? Did the yellow fever he contacted in Cuba and his long recovery effect his thinking? Or was he following the life the cowboy who spent their free time socializing at the bar?

The life of a cowboy was lonely. Working for weeks at a time on the range, the only people they saw were other cowboys and maybe a rancher or two. A day off was a good reason to go to town and "wet the whistle" with a few drinks. Cowboys party hardy, and after long weeks in the saddle, Tom joined in on the fun. On more than on occasion, his "fun" got him into some serious trouble. Sadly, this one he could not get out of.

On Saturday, January 11, 1902, Horn started in Laramie on a drinking binge, took the train to Cheyenne, and caroused all night. Sunday morning, Lefors found Horn in one of the bars and invited him up to his office to talk.

Letters were written between Horn and Lefors about a job in Montana for the Union Pacific. Tom was excited to take it. Thinking this is what was on Lefors' mind, Horn went with him.

What really was on Lefors' mind was to portray Tom as a vicious child killer. He did a fine job of this. The job was a hoax and was used to lure Horn into Lefors' clutches.

Knowing he was going to trick Horn into a confession, he placed Charles Ohnhaus, a stenographer, and Les Snow, a deputy sheriff, into an adjoining room so they could record this "confession."

> **_"I wrote the letters for a good reason, and used them for a good purpose."_**
> Joe Lefors

Lefors previously had a locksmith put a lock on the adjoining door, who fashioned it so the two could see and hear the conversation more easily. They sat on a buffalo robe on the floor by the door and listened to what Tom had to say while Ohnhaus took notes.

In the preface to Tom's autobiography, John Coble strongly pointed out that _Tom never swore!_ (Himself, 1904). He emphasized this point because Tom's confession is riddled with profanity. This is consistent with his testimony in both the inquests and at his trial. He was always polite and never profane. He was feisty when drunk, but people said he was a mild-mannered man (Bowers, 2004).

Using the false job offer as a guise, the conversation turned toward the killing of Willie. Lawman to lawman, Tom told Lefors what he had heard and how he thought the killing happened; which was to repeat the general opinion of the people on Iron Mountain.

Lefors mentioned the killings of other men in previous years, and Tom went right along with the "josh." If he had not been recovering from his weekend of partying, Tom might have been more aware of what Lefors was up to, but he felt at the time they were just sharing war stories. Lefors conned Tom into admitting that he had killed these other men, and Stoll used this to show a pattern during the trial.

Horn and Lefors parted with the understanding that Horn would leave for Montana the next day. Ohnhaus hurried home and "transcribed" his notes. Horn was arrested the next morning at the Inter Ocean hotel.

It is difficult for historians to ascertain how much of this confession is the truth and how much was confabulated, but the transcription of the conversation, correct or not, was enough for prosecutor Walter Stoll. He had his man, and he was going to hang him, whatever it took.

When Deputy Smalley walked Tom from the hotel to the jail, the deputy asked about his height, weight, and age. "I weigh about two hundred pounds... I'm forty-four years, forty-four months, forty-four days, forty-four hours, and forty-four seconds, and I'm six-foot, one inch tall" (Carlson, 2001).

He kept his sense of humor throughout the trial and until the day he died. When he was jailed, he immediately asked to see Lefors. He refused at first, but Smalley convinced him to come. When Horn said they had him in there for killing the kid, Lefors reportedly said, "The hell they have!"

DID HORN KILL THESE MEN?

In case plan A failed, Stoll had a plan B in place. He knew of four men whose murders were associated with Tom Horn. The deaths were not proven, and this was convenient for Stoll, making it easier to pin the deaths on Tom. Lefors mentioned these men when he was squeezing out the confession, and Stoll used them against Horn during the hearing.

The cattlemen knew all settlers were not rustlers, most of them were honest citizens only wanting to start a new life. If there was no need to be afraid, then life went on. But the ones who were rustling would find a note on their door telling them to leave the area or be killed. Most of them left the area. A few did not make it out in time.

William Lewis was a rustler with an unsavory character who had a shady history of stealing personal items and rustling cattle from neighbors in the Iron Mountain area. While being charged with one offense, he was then charged for rustling from the Swan Land and Cattle Company. The prosecutor dropped the first case, and the jury found him not guilty in the case against the Swan Company. He sued four of the partners in the company, including John Coble, for $15,000 for financial damages (equivalent to $300,000 today).

He received notes to stop stealing, move, or be killed. Twice someone shot at him; then his cabin was burned to the ground. He moved further south to Horse Creek but continued his rustling. He was deeply in debt with his legal bills, and his property was mortgaged to the hilt. On July 31, 1895 he was killed by gunshot while loading a stolen skinned beef onto his wagon.

Fred Powell was friends with Lewis. He was a pariah in the community because he got into more trouble with more people than most. He lost an arm as a young man when he worked for the railroad, but despite his handicap, he was good with a rope and horses. He would taunt his neighbors by inviting them to his house for dinner so they could enjoy their beef he had stolen. He had a series of offenses of cattle rustling, destruction of property, grand larceny, and criminal trespass. Most of the charges were either dropped or he was found not guilty. He continued to rustle and steal property. He received letters telling him to stop killing cattle or be killed, or leave the country. He was shot September 10, 1895 while working on his ranch. His ranch hand was the only one present. His wife Mary and son Billy were in Cheyenne.

In 1900, two more men were shot and killed in much the same manner. Brown's Hole, which consists of the area from the towns of Baggs and Saratoga, Wyoming, to Craig, Colorado, was infamous for hiding outlaws, including Butch Cassidy and his gang who lived and worked there.

Tom Horn used the alias Tom Hicks while in Brown's Hole. In the spring of 1900, he was sent there by his employer, Ora Haley, who had a ranch on the Snake River and owned the VD brand. Matt Rash lived in Brown's Hole and was known for stealing and altering brands. Horn worked for Rash for a short time while he investigated the rustling. Isam Dart and Rash were friends and cohorts in the cattle-stealing business. It was said they started out for Rock Springs one day with five or six cows, and by the time they reached their destination, the herd had grown to seventeen or twenty.

Rash accused Dart of taking more than his share of the profits, and an argument ensued. Dart told Rash; Tom Horn witnessed this altercation. He later found two hides stamped with the VD brand in Rash's shed, which he reported to his employer.

Rash received the anonymous letter: sell your cattle and get out of the country or be killed. He was murdered July 8, 1900.

Isam Dart was known for riding with a gang of horse thieves south of Saratoga, Wyoming. The posse in pursuit caught the gang and killed all but Dart. Playing dead until morning, he snuck away and took the loot from the dead men. He stole a horse and the rancher shot him, leaving him for dead, but was found by an accomplice who nursed him back to health. He became known in the area as a horse breaker and all-round cowboy. Horn signed a complaint against Dart in early 1900 as a horse thief.

On October 4, 1900, Dart and five of his friends holed up at Dart's place, afraid they were targets. As the group was moving to the sheds, Dart was killed with a single gunshot. A letter was found near Dart's cabin – move or be killed.

One shell, a .30-30, was found in a grove of aspens where a horse had been tied about 200 yards from where Isam was shot. They also found muddy hoof prints that led away from the tree toward the Snake River. Later a rancher followed those same tracks to Ora Haley's ranch.

WAS THERE A SECOND MAN?

Although Fred Powell's young son, Billy, identified Horn as he man who shot his father, Mary Powell was adamant through the years that Tom Horn did not kill Fred. Horn and Coble were in Bates Hole, a hundred miles away when William Lewis was murdered, so they were cleared there.

As far as killing Matt Rash, when Horn offered his condolences to Rash's brother and father who came up from Texas to get the body. He told them he and Rash were friends, and they had worked together that winter.

Some people thought Isam Dart killed Powell, but when somebody killed Dart, no one was quite sure, and speculation rested on Tom Horn.

The point of Tom's history as an Indian scout, is that he would not be careless enough to leave a spent shell or muddy horse tracks leading him back to his employer's ranch.

Nor would he kill a 14-year-old boy for a $500 diamond. Mary Powell said another man killed her husband, so was there a copycat, or maybe someone working with Horn?

An article in the December 5, 1899 *Steamboat Pilot* presented a theory that the governors of Wyoming, Utah and Colorado were involved in plans to clean out the Hole in the Wall outlaws that hung out in Brown's Hole. The governors had interests against the rustlers and planned to hire a detective to enter that area. The article reported that there was a second man in the area who was not as good a shot as the first.

The second man may have been an acquaintance of Tom's, Bob Melburn. Melburn led an interesting life on both sides of the law. He may have worked for the Pinkerton's at the same time as Horn. Later, he was deputy sheriff in Baggs, Wyoming, when Horn got into a drunken fight with two cowboys who cut his neck with a knife. Melburn watched over Horn until he recovered enough to ride again.

In December 1894, Melburn was sentenced to twenty months in the Deer Lodge, Montana, jail for stealing a saddle. At the time, he was known to be a member of a gang of horse thieves, not the brightest man in the bunch.

Did Melburn work with Horn in Brown's Hole? Was he working under the orders of Tom's employers, and not Horn himself? Is he the shooter that left the sloppy trail? We will never know. Nevertheless, Horn's reputation as a hired assassin, his long days in the saddle with no one to vouch for his whereabouts, his system that never failed, and his weekend of drinking all worked against him and lead to his conviction.

Tom Horn has a terrible reputation for killing many men in cold blood. But when you look at his life before he came to Wyoming, you see an Indian scout, a man trusted by both Indian and military leaders alike; someone who seemed truthful and upright.

What if he was not a killer, what if he was just a man making his place in the world, enjoying life, doing what it took to survive? His job as scout and stock detective were going by way of the cowboy, and perhaps he was thinking about finding a wife and settling down. Psychologists have "examined" his head based their readings of the history books. Was he really the psychopath he is portrayed, and if so, when did he become the cold-blooded killer, and where is the proof other than newspaper reports?

No one knows, but in actuality, no one should have known about him. If the authorities had done their job, had made it their priority to find the guilty man, rather than pick someone out of the crowd and make him pay, we would never have heard of Tom Horn.

He was hanged not because the murder of the boy was fastened up him "beyond peradventure of a reasonable doubt, but on "general principle" that he "had it coming." …Before a shred of testimony was offered he was a doomed man; public opinion had convicted him and intended to have him hanged…The jury returned the verdict…despite the testimony of a physician who performed an autopsy on the Nickell boy that the bullet which killed him was of much greater caliber than those of Horn's gun…"

John Charles Thompson, a Cheyenne newsman who followed Horn's trial from beginning to end

Chapter 12

YOU CAN'T HUNT DUCKS WITH A BRASS BAND

"You can't hunt ducks with a brass band," was Senator Warren's motto. Lefors and Stoll would have done well to take his advice. Acting in his new capacity as private detective for the county, Lefors questioned Mary Nickells. He also interviewed the Miller family in Glendolene's presence. Once again, her study of human nature kicked in and she felt Lefors was up to no good. She warned Tom at the second inquest that Lefors was up to no good, and if Horn had listened to her, he would have been more cautious when Lefors approached him, and perhaps not have gotten into the predicament he was in.

Lefors was not the only one who had high hopes for further career advancement.

Walter Stoll was so confident in hanging the notorious child killer that he scheduled the trial one month before the elections of 1902, in which he was running again for the office of county attorney. If he could win this trial, his future would be set.

Charles Ohnhaus, the stenographer that transcribed Horn's confession, led a long lucrative career as Clerk of the U.S. District Court in Cheyenne.

Governor Chatterton, having been appointed as governor, was looking forward being elected.

> **"Show me a cattleman who is against Tom Horn and I'll show you a rustler!"**
> Glendolene Kimmel
> Himself, 1904

Public opinion was all for hanging Tom Horn, and that is where the political winds were blowing. The people were tired of the rustlings, lynchings, and shootings, and they were ready to see it end. The employers of Horn were cattlemen who owned some of the biggest ranches in the state, and they had not won a case yet. John Coble believed in Tom's innocence, but the rest were not so sure. The cattlemen conducted business underhanded and were afraid Tom would reveal them, so they distanced themselves from him.

Johnathan Bakker, *Tracking Tom Horn,* had this to say (Bowers, 2004):

> "… the death of Willie dropped a perfect opportunity into the laps of the "cattle barons,"…Horn could be blamed for the killing and hung, and they would be forever free, their risk of him telling all he knew about their activity…Horn himself meant little to them – hired guns like him were easy to be had…

> The strategy was remarkably simple. Lefors was enlisted to find or procure evidence against Horn sufficient to have him arrested and charged with the murder. The finest legal defense that money could buy was then retained and set to doing the minimum necessary to believably defend Horn.

An interesting thing about the experts who testified about the bullets that killed Willie. The defense brought in Dr. Samuel Barber who testified that the body was in a highly decomposed state when he examined it, but by the trajectory of the bullets through the body, the boy was standing when he was hit, with the shooter in an outcrop sixty yards away. The boy started to walk for home but fell face first sixty-five yards from where he was shot. The shooter then walked up and turned him over. Dr. Barber testified that the bullets were from a weapon of .38 to .45 caliber, not a .30, and judging from the burns around the wounds, the bullets were consistent with black powder lead bullets and not the new smokeless-powder rounds such as Horn used. This was a big score for the defense.

The next day Stoll was ready to renounce Barber's testimony. Since Barber had testified at the inquest, Stoll was expecting his testimony at the trial. In his fashion of muddying the waters, Stoll brought in four of his own witnesses.

The most damaging testimony was from Pete Bergerson, "a champion rifle shot of the world at 200 yards" (Davis, 2001), which Stoll felt made him a qualified expert on ammunition, guns, and gunshot wounds. Bergeson cast doubt on Dr. Barber's testimony, saying he doubted anyone could tell the difference of the type of gunshot from two miles away. This disparaged the witnesses who said they heard gunshots and identified the type of bullet by sound.

Willie was only three-quarters of a mile from the house, not two miles, but this testimony was enough to cast a shadow on the facts. Interestingly, in a very Stoll-like fashion, Bergerson was the man who changed the locks and refashioned the door in Lefors' office for Tom's confession.

Score another one for Walter Stoll! He cast a shadow of doubt on each of the witnesses for the defense, twisted their testimony, and made a big deal about their truth and veracity.

One of the witnesses, Frank Stone, testified that he had been with Tom in Laramie while he was on his drinking binge the Saturday after Willie's murder. Stoll tried to get Stone to admit that he had sworn a false affidavit saying Horn was with him when Willie had been killed.

Stoll asked Stone if he had not told the justice of the peace that he drank with Tom in Laramie on the Saturday July, 19, 1901, and Stone said, "No sir, I told him where I was when the murder was committed. I told him I was in the Snowy Range. He went so far to state that the Denver newspaper said I was coming here to testify to a false alibi to clear Mr. Horn."

> ***Mr. Stoll, I know a great many men who try to break out of the penitentiary, but not to break in. I said I was a hundred miles away, and I would not swear to a false alibi or anything else.***
> Carlson, 2001

Lefors brought Stoll three witnesses who swore they had seen Tom in a bar during Denver festival days bragging about killing Willie, but Tom had gotten in a fight with a boxer from Denver the night before the festivities. This put Horn in the hospital for three weeks, unable to speak.

> ***I got into trouble because a man called me a liar!***
> Referring to his broken jaw in Denver, September 30, 1901

The testimony of the men was taken word for word from Tom's confession.

> ***"That was the best goddamn shot I ever made, and the dirtiest trick I ever done."***

Judge Scott, who presided over the trial did not want to hear about an alternate suspect. Scott was involved in the change of venue for the invaders of the Johnson County War, in which they were all acquitted. He was clearly not interested in prosecuting anyone but Tom Horn.

Whenever Tom's attorneys brought up the subject of the Millers as suspects, Stoll objected, and the judged sustained. Their hands were tied, there was nothing to be done to get around Walter Stoll and Judge Scott.

Historians and attorneys who have reviewed this case say Horn should never have testified. His ego and his propensity to brag caused his doom. He never admitted to the confession. He admitted to the words he spoke while drunk, because he distinctly remembered saying them, but he thought he and Lefors were "joshing."

Unless you have been accused of wrongdoing and had people lie against you "under oath," you have no idea what it feels like. You sit there helpless, listening to the lies, knowing the judge, jury and public believe them, and there is nothing you can do to take away their words, or change your situation. Imagine sitting in the defendant's chair, knowing full well you did not commit this crime of which you are accused, and have the jury pronounce you guilty, and the judge sentence you to hanging until death.

What would you do? What most innocent, wrongly accused people do. They defend themselves.

Whatever Horn said was twisted and turned against him by County Attorney Stoll. Tom told his story clearly and without malice (or profanities), consistent with his testimony at the coroner's inquest. But according to one of his attorneys, Tom made a fool of himself when he was on the stand the afternoon Stoll cross-examined him. He talked too much.

It was not Tom's ego that caused his doom, but the egos of Joe Lefors and Walter Stoll and their desire for political fame. Tom should have never been tried for Willie's murder, because Lefors' evidence was circumstantial and based on assumptions.

People saw Horn in the area but could never place him at the scene. Not having the means to properly determine which gun shot Willie, it was pure speculation that it was Tom's gun.

A case could be made against the Millers, with the way they sidestepped questions, played down the conflicts, and causally laid blame on others to take the spotlight away from them. The answers between family members were too pat, and Jim was the kind of man that would have coached them in what to say.

Victor did not appeared at the inquests. He was only questioned by Governor Chatterton after Glendolene came forth with her testimony against him.

A deal existed between Lefors and Miller, and Lefors admitted his investigation could have gone the other way.

Horn's reputation, whether it was factual or braggadocio, sealed his fate.

Stoll covered all his bases to make sure he would win this case, including selecting a jury that consisted mostly of rustlers.

A TAMPERED JURY

Smoke and mirrors. Justice is not about accountability, but how attorneys can skew the facts to make their case.

In a 1993 mock trial, Horn was found innocent. The attorneys for the trial said Tom's was one worst cases of defense they had seen. If the defense would have had their day in court, Tom would have been a free man. The closing arguments said it all.

The defense's argument:

1. The prosecution presented weak circumstantial evidence. Horn could not show an alibi because of the nature of his work, and there was no physical evidence that proved he killed Willie.

2. The prosecution never demonstrated a motive.

3. The Denver witnesses were perjured. Horn was in the hospital with a broken jaw. They parroted the newspapers by using the same language as the articles.

4. The firearms experts were scorned by Stoll who called them liars.

5. The confession was tainted by Tom's inebriated state and should be construed as a drunkard's boast.

6. The footprint found by the body was not brought up in the trial. The footprint was a size 7 or 8, the size of a boy or a small man. Tom was six feet, one inch. His shoe size was a ten or eleven. The attorneys had his boots to submit as an exhibit, but never did.

The prosecution's argument:

1. Horn's motive was to keep Willie from running back home and "raising a commotion."

2. Stoll brought in the story of Powell's son identifying Horn as the "man who killed my daddy." This was total conjecture and a mean trick, and he used it to point out that it was the turning point in Horn's thinking. He would never let a kid pinpoint him again.

3. Lefors should be believed, not Horn.

4. Horn took matters into his own hands.

5. Horn was close enough to the area to have committed the crime.

6. Horn's confession was "the last straw of a drowning man."

Several members of the jury, and a waitress at the Inter Ocean Hotel where the jury was sequestered and ate their meals, testified that the public made threatening comments to them. Horn's attorney received a letter signed "not a friend of Horn's" stating that Horn should be "hung as high as they could hang him (Carlson, 2001).

A great-nephew of one of the jurors reported that his father believed money was passed to the jury. My Uncle was so dishonest you could not believe him if he said, 'good morning'. Another juror owned a few cattle and horses valued at $340. In 1905, he sold them to Swan Cattle Company for $2,100. This juror was also on the jury for a similar murder case in Idaho, and had frightened this jury by telling them their families would meet a terrible fate if they brought in a conviction (Carlson, 2001)

Even though women had served on juries since 1871, not one was called for this panel. Starting with a pool of eighty-six men, the numbers were shortly whittled down to thirty-six, and thirteen were chosen within three hours of starting the selection.

Many of the prospective jurors were disqualified after they stated they were less willing to convict for a murder based on circumstantial evidence than for having formed an opinion (Davis, 2016).

> ***Horn and his friends had recovered stolen stock from some of the jury men. The majority of the jury were cattle rustlers!***
> Glendolene Kimmel
> Himself, 1904

Of the thirteen jurors, only three were not cattlemen. There was a Union Pacific porter, a blacksmith, and a butcher. The others were from ranches in the surrounding area; two from the Two-Bar Ranch, the very ranch Tom worked for, and he was friends with both the foreman and the ranch hand.

This was another case of rustlers versus cattlemen, but this cattleman was on his own. The jury retired at 11:25 a.m. on October 24, 1903, and returned a verdict of guilty in the first degree at 4:30 p.m. Two held out for acquittal until the last, including Tom's friend.

But in his closing arguments, Stoll gave them an out by telling them that if they should find Horn guilty, he would have the opportunity to appeal to the Wyoming Supreme Court and then the governor, and with this argument in mind, the jury voted for conviction.

WHERE IS GLENDOLENE?

The defense was so confident in winning their case that they felt bringing the schoolteacher to testify was not necessary. However, they failed in to bring in the Millers as suspects. Stoll and Judge Scott kept that line of questioning away by objecting and sustaining the defense's attempts. Perhaps after realizing what Stoll was up to, Tom's lawyers wished they had brought Glendolene to testify, but she was in Kansas.

> *…men in positions of trust, puffed up with their "little brief authority," who have besmirched their trust and stooped to odious means for their selfish ends…Wyoming politicians play the game of justice with human souls for pawns, and I may add, with Cowardice as referee."*
> John Coble

Stoll wanted Glendolene to testify against Horn, and he sent William Ross to Kansas to find her and offered to pay expenses and "a little extra" if she would come back to Wyoming. She told Ross she was not interested in testifying; she was not going to be coerced into testifying; but she did not tell Ross what she knew about Victor.

"Stoll had said to him unless I took the stand against Tom Horn, they wouldn't have testimony strong enough to convict Tom Horn. Ross further said that Stoll would be terribly angry if I didn't take the stand against Tom Horn, and would probably cause me a great deal of trouble".

> "I made out an affidavit for presentation to the District Court; but owing to my ignorance of the law - solely owing to this - I made out the affidavit in a form too general to be of any use to Tom Horn's attorneys. Before I had time to make out a new affidavit, the time which the law allows for the filing of an affidavit (disclosing new testimony) in the District or the Supreme Court had elapsed."
> Glendolene Kimmel

It was just as well she did not testify. Stoll would have had a great time discrediting her testimony, twisting, and turning the facts like he did with all the other witnesses.

Speculation as to why she did not testify bounced around like a rubber ball. Gossip columnist Polly Pry, the notorious muckraker from the *Denver Post*, did the most damage by publishing her opinion intermingled with facts, swaying the public against Tom and Glendolene. The papers said she was a lover scorned and would come forth and implicate Horn. They said she was starry-eyed-in-love with Tom and would do whatever it took to get him off. They said they saw her in a saloon in Denver, implying she was a prostitute (Bowers, 2004).

During the inquest, Jim and Gus Miller said Horn was sweet on the schoolteacher. Well, maybe he was. They met at breakfast on Tuesday morning, and she and Horn spent time together talking until Tom left on Wednesday. Maybe a spark started between them that would have flared if Tom had been left to live out his life in peace. It must have been a treat for both of them. Horn was from Missouri, just a short distance from where Glendolene grew up. The two days Horn spent at the Millers was the only time they met. There is no indication they ever corresponded.

Glendolene's involvement stemmed from the moral outrage of seeing an innocent man convicted when she knew the truth. At first, like she promised, she gave the Miller's a chance to redeem themselves, but they did not. She told them if an innocent man was convicted, she was coming forth.

In October 1903, after Tom's appeal to the Supreme Court failed, Glendolene came back to Wyoming to see what she could do to save him from the gallows. She spoke with Governor Chatterton and two of the Supreme Court Justices, pleading for Tom's release.

She wrote her affidavit on October 12, 1903, a year after she left Cheyenne, stating what she knew, hoping it would do some good. It did just the opposite. The press had a field day.

Because of her change of testimony from the coroner's inquests to her October 1903 affidavit, Governor Chatterton accused her of presenting "theories" to try to save Horn, and said her affidavit was of no use.

The affidavit that weighed the heaviest against Glendolene in the Governor's decision was from Sheriff H.A. Mendenhall from Kansas City, dated November 13, 1903. He swore that a year before in November of 1902, he had talked to Glendolene at a hotel in Kansas City where she told him a man whose name Mendenhall did not recall was innocent and Horn was guilty. He stated Glendolene said she was willing to go to Cheyenne and testify against Horn, and even went to the trouble of contacting the Laramie County sheriff's office to arrange for transportation. She then changed her mind and decided not to go. When Mendenhall questioned this and told her she would make more as a witness then a schoolteacher, he said she replied, "But suppose the other fellow would give you more than that, what would you do?" (Bowers, 2004). Implying, of course, that she was willing to take money to testify against Horn and her earlier allegations against the Millers were false. This meeting never happened (Bowers, 2004).

Stoll carried out his threat to Glendolene. She made him mad. He set out to cause her a great deal of trouble, just as Ross had warned her. Walter Stoll had her arrested for perjury on November 10, 1903, ten days before Tom was scheduled to be executed. She spent a short time in the same jail as Horn, but Coble and the owner of the Inter Ocean hotel paid her bail ($2000), and she was confined to her room at the hotel until her trial.

A clever way to shut down a witness. With the press convincing the public that she and Tom were in cahoots and she was his lover, and now with her incarceration, she must have been a mess emotionally. She sat in her room, helpless, on November 20, 1903, when Tom was hung. Imagine her despair.

Five days later, Stoll moved to dismiss her charges, stating that he had "reviewed" the law. Perjury could only be committed in court, and lying to the governor did not count. This was his intention. He knew the law, but he had to shut her down, and he did.

Governor Fennimore Chatterton received letters telling him to commute Tom's sentence to life or his career would be over. He received affidavits from Tom's friends telling him he was innocent. The Miller family was ordered to Cheyenne to answer the

> I think that since my coming here the yellow journal reporters are better equipped to write my history than I am myself!
> Tom Horn
> Himself, 1904

allegations made by Glendolene. They denied it all, but it was doubtful that anyone but Victor and Jim, and maybe Gus, knew anything about Victor killing Willie. The governor questioned Victor at length, who denied any involvement.

The press speculated that Tom's employers were nervous because they felt he would tell all and reveal their secrets. If there were secrets, Tom took them to his death, but it is unlikely he had anything to implicate them with. Could it be that he was never a hired assassin, and that his job was to take care of the rustlers in an orderly fashion that did not involve the courts, but also did not involve killing? He never spoke of his employers, but he had a lot to say about Lefors and Ohnhaus!

In an October 3, 1903 letter to Ohnhaus: "Now, sir, I am going to make an appeal to you to act on my behalf, and it certainly is not much that I ask – only that you make an affidavit to the facts in this supposed confession of mine" (Carlson, 2001).

> At his trial, Tom testified, "You put in your report that I said: 'That was the best shot I ever made, and the dirtiest trick I ever did.' You and I, and the others I have mentioned, know that was made up by Stoll or Lefors, and put in the notes by you."

October 3, 1903, Horn wrote to his friend and benefactor, John Coble:

> That conversation in the marshal's office was all changed to meet the requirements and Ohnhaus would hardly go back on it now. I don't know why (illegible) would be to try and get the Governor to cut the sentence down to life imprisonment and wait for Snow or Ohnhaus to get around to tell the truth. They will tell it sometime, but I can't benefit by it much if they tell it all after I am hanged.

One-hundred and twenty years later, the truth of Tom Horn is finally told.

FAILED APPEALS

Although there was extensive testimony and affidavits made by both sides, nearly all statements made by the witnesses were countered and contradicted by the testimony of another. There are documents supporting the charges and countercharges of all the witnesses except Glendolene's testimony. Every piece of evidence regarding her testimony has been removed from her case file. The only thing remaining, where her affidavit should be, is a copy of one of her hurried requests to friends in Missouri asking to testify to her veracity and chastity (Bowers, 2004).

However, historian Chip Carlson printed Glendolene's October 3, 1903 affidavit in both his out-of-print book on Lefors, and again in *"Tom Horn. Blood on the Moon. Dark history of the murderous cattle detective."* It is unknown where this affidavit came from, considering the documents from the trial are missing. Glendolene's affidavit consistent with her 1904 narrative published with Horn's book *"The Life of Tom Horn, Government Scout and Interpreter"* written by Himself.

One part, item #4, arises suspicion because the writing style suddenly changes, and the tone is inconsistent with the rest of her narrative. "I know Tom Horn very well and understand his nature perfectly." She talked about his drinking, and stated, "many times I have been with Tom Horn when he was drunk." "When Tom Horn was at the Miller Ranch, I heard James Miller tell Tom Horn the identical tale about the murders of Lewis and Powell that Tom Horn repeated to Lefors." More along this line, and then in item #5, resumes her style of narrative. It is well documented that the only time she saw Tom was at the Millers and at the inquests. She did not know him "very well" or spend time with him when he was drunk.

Considering the botched acquisition of Horn's confession, it does not take much of an imagination to suspect Stoll of adding item #4 to discredit Glendolene and to further cement the case. With this included into her affidavit, it is no wonder Governor Chatterton disqualified her testimony.

Stoll boasted that he would prosecute everyone who wrote false affidavits testifying in Horn's behalf, but Glendolene was the only one he arrested.

One of Tom's attorneys, Edward T. Clark, signed a statement swearing that on February 11, 1903, Clark and Lefors were in the smoking compartment of a train going to Alliance, Nebraska. Lefors told Clark that "Stoll had advised the county commissioners not to pay Lefors' the award money until the appeal had been decided by the Supreme Court," and this was Stoll's way of keeping Lefors in line. "Stoll had better be careful how he treated him since he knew Lefors had knowledge of evidence which would clear Tom Horn. He said that if he had been working on the other side of the case, he would have cleared Tom Horn" (Carlson, 2001).

Chatterton should have listened to the threats because the Warren Machine was in full power, and it was aimed at Chatterton's career. Before he became Secretary of State, from where he was appointed governor when the former governor died, he had a falling out with his law partner. David Craig quit the firm because he felt Chatterton was unduly sympathetic to the cattlemen. The final blow came when Craig suspected Chatterton of taking a bribe in the lynching of Cattle Kate and Jim Averel in July, 1989.

Chatterton was popular with the public, especially now that he had put an assassin away. This was his first campaign as governor. Or so he thought. He never made it to the ballot – the Republican Convention put another in his place. His political career came to a screeching halt.

Mendenhall came out smelling like a rose. He and Chatterton were both leaders in the Republican party; Chatterton lost out, but Mendenhall advanced. Shortly before his affidavit, he was elected as Sheriff for the fifth term. Two months later, he resigned his position, and within a year surfaced as a major stockholder (with a sheriff's salary) for the Home State Bank in Kansas City. The next year, he became the president of the bank (Bowers, 2004).

Lefors, thinking his great arrest would advance his career, was fooled as well. He wrote in his autobiography that he lost all backing from the U.S. Marshall officers. In June 12, 1903, he resigned his post with the U.S. Marshall's office and assigned his reward over to his supervisor, Frank Hadsell, requesting that he send his wife $100 a month from his pay. He wrote a letter to his wife postmarked June 15, 1903 from Cape Gracias a Dios, Nicaragua (Carlson, 2001).

Lefors wrote a long-winded letter to Hadsell dated September 21, 1903, telling about his work in Nicaragua and asking about the Horn case. Did Lefors leave the country because he was afraid something bad would happen to him? When he came back to Wyoming, he continued working in law enforcement, but he never made the great heights he anticipated when he agreed to the $1000 reward. He must have felt guilty because he returned the money.

Glendolene never married. She lived as a spinster in California with her mother. They were so poor, she wrote to relatives in Missouri for money to bury her mother. Could it be that the onslaught of shame brought on by her ordeal in Wyoming never left her?

John Coble, Horn's friend and employer that supported him to the end, failed financially because of the legal expenses incurred during the trial. He committed suicide in a hotel lobby in Elko, Nevada, in 1914.

Walter Stoll won the election and went on to be an acclaimed as an attorney, but he never made his dream of Supreme Court Justice. He died of alcoholism and heart failure in 1911.

After Willie was killed and Kels was shot, the Nickells sold the farm and moved to Cheyenne.

Kels Nickells sold his ranch and moved to Cheyenne shortly after Willie died. He lost his ranch, his son had been murdered, and his livelihood was gone. Jim Miller bought the Nickells' ranch and was considered a well-to-do and respected neighbor on Iron Mountain.

Jennie Tupper worked for Judge Lacey, Horn's lead defense, as his private secretary. Except for one occasion, Aunt Jennie would never talk about the Tom Horn case, even in the closed circles of our family.

The occasion when Tupper broke her silence was after listening to a radio broadcast with her nephews from Denver's KOA station on Wyoming history that covered the Tom Horn affair. "You know, boys, Tom Horn never killed Willie Nickell" (Carlson, 2001).

Who is the criminal? Tom Horn, or the state that wrongfully convicted him? Does murder take on a different face when it is ordered by the law? A lynching is a lynching, whether by vigilantes or a governor's decree.

The tactics used by Stoll and Lefors are still used today, and this is why there are innocent people in prisons and jails. Where is the accountability for those who enforce the law? Where are the checks and balances to prevent this from happening?

If you have never been on the receiving end of lies, it may be difficult to image what it is like. Straight-faced liars are the worst. They say anything people want to hear and have a poker face and non-lying eyes when they say it. The non-lying eyes are what put innocent people behind bars. Some people lie for a living. If you do not conform to their way of thinking, they will do whatever they can to belittle and denigrate you. And the worst thing about liars? They muddy the truth, so no one knows the real story.

You know. How could you not know you murdered someone? You say you did not do it: they say you did. We believe in the court system to sort out the guilty, but perhaps we should be more like Tom Horn and trust cattle more than courts.

The Millers appeared as innocents, but if you examine their testimony from a lying point of view, you will see their stories match – down to what was eaten for breakfast the morning Willie was shot. Too much useless information. The family had their story straight from the first coroner's inquest, and never wavered from that.   Consistency appears as truthfulness, when in fact, such tight consistency between witnesses is a sure indication someone is lying. If their stories match to a T, then the "T" they are crossing is most certainly not the truth.

If Glendolene did not have these conversations with the Millers, then why did she suddenly quit her job and leave town? She was afraid. She found information after she testified at the inquest, but by the time she came forward, no one wanted to hear it.

But then, it may not have made a difference if she had told Stoll before she left Wyoming. The wheels against Tom Horn had already been set in motion.

This is why conspiracies exist. We tend to believe the majority and those in authority. If a judge makes a ruling, it must be fair. If more people say it is true than those who say it is false, then it must be true. This is human nature, and this thinking works well for the scammers and liars.

Criminals will not admit their wrongdoing but lay the blame on others. This is what gets innocent people in trouble. They too, sound like they are blaming others, but in their case, it is not blame, but telling the truth. "Please listen to me." We should be more discerning about who we believe, and why. Everyone is not guilty; most people are honest citizens just trying to live a good life.

To further their non-truths, liars attack our vulnerability and faith in human nature, and our desire to do the right thing. Judges, lawyers, and policemen pride themselves in sifting out this criminal thinking. They have the "facts," but can become blind-sided by those facts. Once their mind is closed to other options, we have a Walter Stoll situation. It is sad that an attorney can knowingly skew the facts and convince a panel of twelve people who strongly believe in their American duty and are committed to ferreting out the truth. They think they are hearing the truth, when they are like sheep, following the leader.

How many ways can you say, "I did not commit this crime," before people hear you? Once they decide otherwise, this is a foreign phrase people do not comprehend.

What do you do? With an estimated 230,000 innocent people behind bars, and an impossible-to-count number of innocent people on probation and parole, the wrongly accused obviously are not alone.

It is up to American to counteract the negativity brought on by the Walter Stolls of the world. The people in power who do what they please without thought of the consequences on others. If you do not like what you see, stand up and be counted! When the citizens speak up without fear of recrimination and tell their stories of mistreatment, judicial reform will occur. And not until then. As long as we stay quiet, the massive incarcerations will continue.

Now that we have finished our journey and beheld the lay of the land behind America's Iron Curtain, what do you think? Is there a connection between suicide, incarceration, and poverty?

"…with liberty and justice for all…"

ACKNOWLEDGEMENTS

A huge thank you to my family for their patience in the long hours of my mental absences while researching and writing this book.

Also, heartfelt gratitude to the authors who made possible this rendition of the story of Tom Horn. There are several accounts of Tom's life, but the research for my book came mostly from Chip Carlson's book, *Tom Horn, Blood on the moon. Dark history of the murderous cattle detective.* Mr. Carlson's twenty years of uncovering the story as told by the historians before him, the many interviews of people who lived on Iron Mountain, and sifting the facts from fiction, helped make the research for this book much easier. John Davis, author of *The Trial of Tom Horn,* was helpful with his legal points of view and knowledge of court procedure.

Sometimes you pick up a book and it opens to exactly what you need, and that is how the story was picked for this book. The saga of Tom Horn was related in an article in an old college textbook, "Readings in Wyoming History. Issues in the history of the equality state." The article was entitled *School Bells and Winchesters: The sad saga of Glendolene Myrtle Kimmell,* published three years after Carlson's book. Ms. Bower touched a chord as she brought to light Glendolene's struggle, and from this account the story for my book was born.

My degrees are a Bachelor of Science Social Science from the University of Wyoming and a master's in healthcare administration from Bellevue University, Nebraska. Because of my legal predicament, writing passes the time while my stalkers keep me captive. Except for *Take the Quantum Leap into Abundance: A guide to the good life,* my books are about society's violence, the causes, and prevention. My first book was on the shelf for 15 years before it was published and is a result of my experience teaching women's self-defense classes, but the other three started with the idea of writing a book on "don't talk to cops!" The research did not lend to that subject as much as what happens when you do talk to cops.

My books can be found at cwpickett.com.

Walking Between the Raindrops: A treatise on trauma. Why women stay with abusive men, Dale Carnegie tips for getting along, a history of society's violence beginning with the Romans.

Take the Quantum Leap into Abundance. A guide to the good life. My idea of what abundance looks like based on people like Admiral Stockdale and the Okinawans.

Seven Summers of Stalking: The #1 crime against women. Written for the benefit of my stalkers and the 7.5 million Americans a year who are stalked.

Beat a Bully without a Fight. Advice for parents. How to keep your child from being bullied, and what to do if she is.

REFERENCES

Ahlberg, B. *U.S. Single Parent Households.* Commission on police standards and training. lib.post.ca.gov/Publications/Building%20a%20Career%20Pipeline%20Documents/Safe_Harbor.pdf

Aiken, J. (2017). *Era of Mass Expansion: Why state officials should fight jail growth.* Prison Policy Initiative. https://www.prisonpolicy.org/reports/jailsovertime.html

Alzheimer's Statistics. (2017). *2017 Alzheimer's Statistics.* Alzheimer's.net. https://www.alzheimers.net/resources/alzheimers-statistics/

American Fact Finder. *Grandchildren characteristics.* 2013-2017 American Community Survey 5-Year Estimate. American Fact Finder. U.S. Census Bureau. https://factfinder.census.gov/faces/tableservices/jsf/pages/productview.xhtml?pid=ACS_17_5YR_S1001& prodType=table

Annie E. Casey Foundation. (2016). *A Shared Sentence. The devasting toll of parental incarceration on kids, families, and communities.* Policy Report. Kids Count. https://www.aecf.org/resources/a-shared-sentence/

Beck, A.J. PhD, Harrison, P.M. (2001). *Prisoners in 2000.* Bureau of Justice Statistics Bulletin. U.S. Department of Justice. Office of Justice Programs. Bureau of Justice Statistics. Washington, D.C. Bureau of Justice Statistics Bulletin. U.S. Department of Justice. Office of Justice Programs. Bureau of Justice Statistics. Washington, D.C.

Becker-Weiderman, A. (2009). Effects of Early Maltreatment on Development: A Descriptive Study Using the Vineland Adaptive Behavior Scales-II. *Child Welfare 88(2),* 137-161. Retrieved from http://search.proquest.com.ezproxy.bellevue.edu/docview/213806844

Bowers, C.L. (2004). *School Bells and Winchesters: The sad saga of Glendolene Myrtle Kimmel.* Readings from Wyoming history: Issues in the history of the equality state. 4th ed. Roberts, P., Editor. Laramie, WY. Skyline Press West/Wyoming Almanac.

Broderick, P.C. & Blewitt, P. (2010). *The life span: Human development of helping professionals.* 3rd. Ed. USA. Pearson.

Bronson, J. PhD., Carson, E.A., PhD. (2019). *Prisoners in 2017.* Bureau of Justice Statistics Bulletin. U.S. Department of Justice. Office of Justice Programs. Bureau of Justice Statistics. Washington, D.C.

Brown, J. (2001). *The link between early learning and care and school readiness.* Economic Opportunity Institute. http://www.opportunityinstitute.org/wp-content/uploads/early-learning/ELCLinkSchooReadiness-Oct02.pdf

Carlson, C. (2001). *Tom Horn. Blood on the moon. Dark history of the murderous cattle detective.* Meeteetse, WY. High Plains Press.

Childcare Capacity in Wyoming. (2017). Annie E. Casey Foundation Kids Count Data Center. https://datacenter.kidscount.org/data/tables/3562-child-care-capacity?loc=52&loct=2#detailed/5/7113-7135/false/871,870,573,869,36,868,867,133,38,35/any/7328

Children and families of the incarcerated fact sheet. National Resource Center on Children & Families of the Incarcerated. Rutgers University, Camden.

Community facts. (2019). American Fact Finder. United Census Bureau.
https://factfinder.census.gov/faces/nav/jsf/pages/community_facts.xhtml

Community Opportunity Map. *Local Data on Community Health to Support Safe Children and Strong Families.*
Casey Family Programs. caimaps.info/caseyfamily/Home

Couloute, L., Kopf, D. (2018). *Out of prison & out of work: Unemployment among formerly incarcerated
people.* Prison Policy Initiative. https://www.prisonpolicy.org/reports/outofwork.html#fnref:13

Criminal Justice Fact Sheet. (2016). National Association for the Advancement of Colored People.
https://www.naacp.org/criminal-justice-fact-sheet/

Curtain, S.C., M.A., Hedegaard, H., M.D., M.S.P.H. (2019). *Suicide rates for females and males by race and
ethnicity: United States, 1999 and 2017.* Health E-Stats. National Center for Health Statistics.
Centers for Disease Control and Prevention.
https://www.cdc.gov/nchs/data/hestat/suicide/rates_1999_2017.pdf

Data USA: Explore, map, compare, and download USA data. www.datausa.io

David-Ferdon, C., Vivolo-Kantor, A. M., Dahlberg, L. L., Marshall, K. J., Rainford, N. & Hall, J. E. (2016). A
Comprehensive Technical Package for the Prevention of Youth Violence and Associated Risk
Behaviors. Atlanta, GA: National Center for Injury Prevention and Control, Centers for Disease
Control and Prevention.

Davis, J.W. (2016). *The trial of Tom Horn.* Norman, OK. University of Oklahoma Press.

Dillinger, J. (2019). *The most dangerous states in the United States.* World Atlas.
https://www.worldatlas.com/articles/the-most-dangerous-states-in-the-u-s.html

Drapeau, C.W. & McIntosh, J.L. (2018). *U.S.A. suicide 2017: Official Final data.* Washington, DC. American
Association of Suicidology. https://www.suicidology.org

Drug War Statistics. (2019) Drug Policy Alliance Headquarters. NY. www.drugpolicy.org/issues/drug-war-
statistics

Facts about suicide among women veterans: August 2017. U.S. Department of Veterans Affairs. Office of
Mental Health and Suicide Prevention. https://www.mentalhealth.va.gov/docs/VA-Women-Veterans-
Fact-Sheet.pdf

Facts about the over-incarceration of women in the United States. (2019). American Civil Liberties Union.
https://www.aclu.org/other/facts-about-over-incarceration-women-united-states

FAQs About Children of Prisoners. Prison Fellowship. https://www.prisonfellowship.org/wp-
content/uploads/2014/03/FAQs-About-Children-of-Prisoners.pdf

Felitti, V., Anda, R., Nordenberg, D., Williamson, D., Spitz, A., Edwards, V., . . . Marks, J. (1998). *Relationship
of childhood abuse and household dysfunction to many of the leading causes of death in adults.*
American Journal of Preventive Medicine *(14)*4, 245-258. Retrieved from
http://search.proquest.com.ezproxy.bellevue.edu/docview/218184173

Fort Peck Community Health Assessment. (2016). Fort Peck Tribes. https://mthcf.org/wp-
content/uploads/2018/01/Fort-Peck-CHA.pdf

Glaze, L.E., Maruschak, L.M. (2008). *Parents in Prison and their Minor Children.* Bureau of Justice Statistics
Special Report. U.S. Department of Justice. Office of Justice Programs. Revised 3/30/10.

Gould. L.L. (1989). *Wyoming. From Territory to Statehood.* Worland, WY. High Plains Publishing Company.

Graham, A. (2019). *Woman's prison conditions like 'stockyard' say former inmates.* WyoFile. https://www.wyofile.com/womens-prison-conditions-like-stockyard-say-former-inmates/

Grandchildren characteristics. 2013-2017 American Community Survey 5-Year Estimate. American Fact Finder. U.S. Census Bureau. https://factfinder.census.gov/faces/tableservices/jsf/pages/productview.xhtml?pid=ACS_17_5YR_S100 1&prodType=table

Haber, E., Flagg, A. (2018). *How incarcerated parents are losing their children forever.* The Marshall Project. https://www.themarshallproject.org/2018/12/03/how-incarcerated-parents-are-losing-their-children-forever

Health of those who have served report 2018. America's Health Rankings. United Health foundation. https://www.americashealthrankings.org/explore/annual/state/AK

Henry, J., Watt, R., Rosenthal, L., Shivji, A. (2016). *The 2016 Annual Homeless Assessment Report (AHAR) to Congress, November 2016. Part 1: Point-in-time estimates of homelessness.* The U.S. Department of Housing and Urban Development. https://files.hudexchange.info/resources/documents/2016-AHAR-Part-1.pdf

Himself. (1904). *Life of Tom Horn. Government scout and interpreter.* John Coble copyright.

Holleran, L. & Poon, G. PhD. *Dying in the Shadows: Suicide among the Homeless.* Harvard Public Health Review. www.harvardpublichealthreview.org/lori

Horvath, J., & Frost, R. (2014). *Incarceration in Wyoming. 2013 Report on Prison and Jail Complaints.* American Civil Liberties Union of Wyoming. https://www.aclu-wy.org/sites/default/files/field_documents/2013_incarceration_wyoming_1.pdf

Joiner, T., PhD. (2007). *Why people die by suicide.* Florida State University. https://dmh.mo.gov/docs/mentalillness/joinerpresentation.pdf

Jones, A. (2018). *Correctional control: 2018. Incarceration and supervision by state.* Prison Policy Initiative. https://www.prisonpolicy.org/reports/correctionalcontrol2018.html

Kajstura, A., Immarigeon, R. *States of Women's Incarceration: The global context.* Prison Policy Initiative. https://www.prisonpolicy.org/global/women/

Kaplan, M.S., Huguet, N., McFarland, B.H., Newsom, J.T. (2007). *Suicide among male veterans: a prospective population-based study.* Journal of Epidemiol Community Health 2007; 61: 619-624.doi: 10.1136/jech.2006.054346 https://www.ncbi.nlm.nih.gov/pmc/articles/PMC2465754/pdf/619.pdf

Kids Count Data Book (2018). *State Trends in Child Well-Being.* Annie E. Casey Foundation. https://www.aecf.org/m/resourcedoc/aecf-2018kidscountdatabook-2018.pdf

Kids Count Data Center. (2019) Annie E. Casey Foundation. https://datacenter.kidscount.org/data

Kilgore, James. (2015). *Jails: Time to wake up to mass incarceration in your neighborhood.* Portside. https://portside.org/2015-03-16/jails-time-wake-mass-incarceration-your-neighborhood

Kovner, A.R., PhD, & Knickman, J.R. PhD. (Eds.). (2008). Jonas and Kovner's Health Care Delivery in the United States (9th Ed.). NY. Springer Publishing Company.

NISVS: An overview of 2010 Findings on victimization by sexual orientation. The National Institute Partner and Sexual Violence Survey. Centers for Disease Control and Prevention. https://www.cdc.gov/violenceprevention/pdf/cdc_nisvs_victimization_final-a.pdf

Nome, Alaska. City-Data.com www.city-data.com/city/Nome-Alaska.html

Northwest Arctic Borough. https://www.nwabor.org/about/

Offenses. (2019). Federal Bureau of Prisons. Statistics.
>	https://www.bop.gov/about/statistics/statistics_inmate_offenses.jsp

Overview of the problem: Suicide and self-harm in correctional facilities. (2019). Vera.
>	https://www.vera.org/publications/culture-of-safety-sentinel-event-suicide-self-harm-correctional-facilities/culture-of-safety/overview

Quick Facts. United States. (2019). https://www.census.gov/quickfacts/fact/table/US/PST045218

Rabuy, B., Kopf, D. (2016). *Detaining the poor.* Prison Policy Initiative. MA. www.prisonpolicy.org

Radley, D.C., McCarthy, D., Hayes, S.L. (2018). *2018 Scorecard on State Health System Performance.* The Commonwealth Fund. https://interactives.commonwealthfund.org/2018/state-scorecard/files/Radley_State_Scorecard_2018.pdf

Reichert, J., Adams, S., Bostwick, L. (2010). *Victimization and help-seeking behaviors among female prisoners in Illinois.* Illinois Criminal Justice Information Authority. www.icjia.state.il.us

Richardson, N., Chermayeff, C., White, A. (Eds). (1992). *Malcolm speaks out.* Kansas City, MO: Andrews and McMeel

Rodriguez, M. N., Emsellem, M. (2011). *65 million need not apply. The case for reforming background checks for employment.* The National Employment Law Project. https://www.nelp.org/wp-content/uploads/2015/03/65_Million_Need_Not_Apply.pdf

Sauter, M.B. (2018). *Faces of poverty: What racial, social groups are more likely to experience it?* US Today. https://www.usatoday.com/story/money/economy/2018/10/10/faces-poverty-social-racial-factors/37977173/

Sawe, B. E. (2019). *U.S. states with the highest suicide rates.* World Atlas. https://www.worldatlas.com/articles/states-with-the-highest-suicide-rates-in-us.html

Sawyer, W., Wagner, P. (2019). *Mass Incarceration: The whole pie 2019.* Prison Policy Initiative. https://www.prisonpolicy.org/reports/pie2019.html

Sawyer, W. (2018). *The Gender Divide: Tracking women's state prison growth.* Prison policy Initiative. https://www.prisonpolicy.org/reports/women_overtime.html

Serious Mental Illness (SMI) prevalence in jails and prisons. (2016). A background paper from the Office of Research & Public Affairs. Criminalization. Treatment Advocacy Center. https://www.treatmentadvocacycenter.org/component/content/article/220-learn-more-about/3695-serious-mental-illness-prevalence-in-jails-and-prisons-

Shaw, B.E. (2019). *States with the highest suicide rates. (2019).* Worldatlas. https://www.worldatlas.com/articles/states-with-the-highest-suicide-rates-in-us.html

Sodaro, C., Adams, R. (1996). *Frontier spirit. The story of Wyoming.* 2nd E. Boulder, CO. Johnson Books.

Stats of the States. National Center for Health Statistics. Centers for Disease Control and Prevention. https://www.cdc.gov/nchs/pressroom/stats_of_the_states.htm

Suicide clusters within American Indian and Alaskan Native Communities: A review of the literature and recommendations. U.S. Department of Health and Human Services. Substance Abuse and Mental Health Services Administration.

Swavola, K. R., Subramanian, R. (2016). *Overlooked: Women and jails in an era of reform.* NY. Vera Institute of Justice.

Tai-Seale, M., McGuire, T. G., & Zhang, W. (2007). Time allocation in primary care office visits. Health services research, 42(5), 1871–1894. doi:10.1111/j.1475-6773.2006.00689.x

USA Health Rankings. (2018). *Deaths by age and gender.* https://www.worldlifeexpectancy.com/usa/wyoming-suicide?order=0'

Van Nuys, D. PhD. *Suicide. An interview with Thomas Joiner, PhD. On why people commit suicide.* Gulf Bend Center. https://www.gulfbend.org/poc/view_doc.php?type=doc&id=29060

Zeng, Z. (2019). *Jail Inmates in 2017.* U.S. Department of Justice. Office of Justice Programs. Bureau of Justice Statistics.